In 1996, conspiracy lectur employee Phil Schneider was ment. Although it is against th ~~detective~~ on the scene did not call the coroner and released the body to the morgue. To his surprise and dismay, the mortician discovered a murder weapon wrapped around the neck of the corpse. The former wife of Phil Schneider was outraged by these circumstances and sought to uncover the truth about her ex-husband's demise but was countered or tricked by the authorities at every step.

An investigation of this covered-up murder revealed astonishing information, the trail of which led back to the infamous Philadelphia Experiment of 1943. Before his assassination, Phil Schneider had lectured across the country and had released documents connecting his father to the U.S.S. Eldridge. Additionally, his father claimed to be a Nazi U-boat captain who, after being captured by the Allies, was recruited as a medical doctor and served as a Senior Medical Officer to the crew of the Eldridge. More haunting was the discovery of gold bars with Nazi insignias in his father's possessions.

The Philadelphia Experiment Murder investigates these circumstances and uncovers a host of new characters, including Preston Nichols' boss from the Montauk Project. Besides exposing the murder of an innocent man, the effort to murder the truth is exposed which leads to an examination of the nature of insanity and its relationship to physics and the constructs of the physical universe itself. In the name of a martyred man, the quantum potential of mankind is opened to a new horizon.

Cover Art:

Artist's depiction of a quantum murder, specifically the murder of quantum consciousness as it relates to the Philadelphia Experiment and all the various concepts and eventualities that it precipitated.

THE PHILADELPHIA EXPERIMENT MURDER

PARALLEL UNIVERSES AND THE PHYSICS OF INSANITY

BY ALEXANDRA BRUCE
EDITED BY PETER MOON

SkyBooks

NEW YORK

Edited by Peter Moon
Cover art and illustration by Ariel Phoenix
Typography by Creative Circle Inc.
Published by: Sky Books
            Box 769
            Westbury, New York 11590
            email: skybooks@yahoo.com
            websites: www.time-travel.com/skybooks
            www.chica.bruce.net

Library of Congress Cataloging-in-Publication Data

Bruce, Alexandra
        The Philadelphia Experiment Murder: Parallel
Realities and the Physics of Insanity
by Alexandra Bruce
        256 pages
        ISBN 0-9631889-5-X
1. Time Travel 2. Mind Control 3. Parallel Universes
Library of Congress Catalog Card Number 00-135081

This book is dedicated to Phil Schneider.
May the memory of his life and death
stir others to seek and find the truth.

ACKNOWLEDGEMENTS

David Anderson
Marshall Barnes
Bob Beckwith
Al Bielek
Cynthia Drayer
Bob Beckwith
Joan D'Arc
Joseph Matheny
Ron Patton
Ariel Phoenix
Glenn Pruitt
Jack Pruitt
Dave Sokolin
Stewart Swerdlow
Kenn Thomas
Val Valerian
Veronica Vostinak

CONTENTS

Other titles from
Sky Books

by Preston Nichols and Peter Moon
The Montauk Project: Experiments in Time
Montauk Revisited: Adventures in Synchronicity
Pyramids of Montauk: Explorations in Consciousness
Encounter in the Pleiades: An Inside Look at UFOs
The Music of Time

by Peter Moon
The Black Sun: Montauk's Nazi-Tibetan Connection

by Stewart Swerdlow
Montauk: The Alien Connection
The Healer's Handbook: A Journey Into Hyperspace

INTRODUCTION

Many years ago, I had learned about the Schneider family from Wilsonville, Oregon and their connection to the Philadelphia Experiment. Phil Schneider was the name of a man who had been lecturing across the country and telling incredible tales about underground bases of the military. He also claimed that his father, Oscar or Otto, had been a Nazi U-boat captain who had shifted his loyalties to the Allies where he served as a full-fledged medical doctor. He had also been seen aboard the *U.S.S. Eldridge*, the ship believed to have been involved in the Philadelphia Experiment

When I first heard of the death of Phil Schneider, I was amazed at the suspicious circumstances surrounding his death. I wanted to investigate the matter and write a book on it. As is the case with so many books I would like to write, time and circumstances would not allow it. Nevertheless, the story stood out and needed to be told.

When I first became involved in the research of the Montauk Project and the Philadelphia Experiment, Preston Nichols told me that it was the martyrizing of Dr. Morris K. Jessup which gave impact and credibility to the original investigation of the secret experiments of 1943. In other words, had he not died and "spilled his blood," there might not have been enough interest generated to find out much at all about the Philadelphia Experiment. For those of you who are not familiar with Morris Jessup, he was a well known scientist and investigator of the paranormal who was discovered dead under suspicious circumstances after being personally responsible for breaking the story which is now known as the Philadelphia Experiment.

At this writing, forty-four years since Jessup was found dead, a new martyr has been created in what I have termed the second "Philadelphia Experiment Murder." An investigation into his death has resulted in a fountain of new information. But, before we go into the details of Phil Schneider and his mysterious death, it will serve us to review the original pattern of how the Philadelphia Experiment sprouted into consciousness in the first place.

After writing an extensive and well thought out book about UFO phenomena entitled *The Case for the UFO*, Morris Jessup became the recipient of very strange mail from Carlos Allende, a mysterious and elusive man who was a witness to the Philadelphia Experiment. In modern folklore and literature, Carlos Allende is the original source or "portal" responsible for unleashing the flow of information which has since ensued. Thus, in the stream of time, there are two major events which resulted in the inception of the Philadelphia Experiment story or legend.

First, there were the letters from Allende. Although Jessup received them over a lengthy period of time, they had a profound impact on him. Allende also sent a cryptically annotated version of Jessup's book to the Navy. This eventually resulted in the Navy contacting Jessup whereupon they actually published it in a limited edition and new format that included Allende's cryptic notes which alluded to UFO propulsion drives being connected to the Unified Field Theory and its application in the so-called Philadelphia Experiment.

Upon being interviewed by the Office of Naval Research several times, Dr. Jessup knew he was coming closer and closer to the truth. But, the more he found out, the more it seemed to disturb him. He commented on a strange pattern of coincidences that seemed to be overwhelming him. After visiting publishers and several friends in New York, he disappeared in 1958 when he was supposed to return to his home in Indiana. After many inquiries were made, he was finally found dead in a car outside of his home in Coral Gables, Florida in what was officially claimed to be a suicide. None of his true friends accepted this and inquiries into the official investigation left many unanswered questions. The obvious conclusion by serious investigators was that he was murdered. The Philadelphia Experiment legend has since grown into several books and a full length motion picture. It has also attracted a steady following of supporters. In fact, it can even be considered that the Philadelphia Experiment legend has reached epic proportions if you consider it all began with a few crack pot letters from Carlos Allende.

When Carlos Allende died in a Colorado nursing home in the early 1990's, there were many questions left unanswered. He left this world with many serious researchers scratching their heads. Anyone who has studied the Philadelphia Experiment to any serious extent knows well that there have been many attempts to pin Carlos Allende down with regard to where he was and what his role was in 1943. Some say that he really wasn't on this ship or that ship. There are also the smug observations that he could not possibly have any real scientific training or acumen because he did not know how to spell or speak good English. There are various theories and assertions as to exactly what he was doing, but none of them are really too important. Too many "head-scratching" researchers have missed the main point of Carlos Allende and his role in releasing the Philadelphia Experiment information. Although it appears in books on the subject, the primary fact of the entire matter has been woefully understated. The following quotations are in his own handwriting from the letters he wrote to Dr. Jessup.

> "I can be of some positive help to you in myself but to do so would require a Hypnotist, Sodium Pentothal, a tape recorder & an excellent typist-secretary in order to produce material of <u>Real</u> value to you."

> "UNDER NARCO-HYPNOSIS I CAN BE ENABLED TO DIVULGE THE NAME, DATE & SECTION & PAGE NUMBER of that Paper & the other one. <u>Thus</u> this Papers "Morgue" will divulge EVEN MORE POSITIVE PROOF ALREADY PUBLISHED of this experiment."

The paper Allende is referring to is what he terms a "Philadelphia NEWSPAPER." Whether this is a screen memory of reading the information from a newspaper or an actual memory, I have no idea. According to sailors at Philadelphia during the time of the experiment, there was an account of the Philadelphia Experiment, at least about a bar room brawl, in a Navy publication named *The Beacon*. Even so, Allende's accuracy is not terribly significant. What is important is that he was aware of sodium-pentothal at all. This was a "truth serum" drug that the Navy experimented with during the war. By placing a subject under the influence of this drug, the operator could find out the most amazing details about his life. There seemed to be no limits to what could be discovered or accomplished with this mental research. Whether as a victim, researcher, or perpetrator trying to clear his guilty conscious, Allende knew about the cutting edge of mind control research. He was hoping that Jessup could help him in this regard. This is the most important point about Carlos Allende and is all we really need to know. For whatever reason and in whatever manner, Allende was a witness to something that completely horrified him. Subsequently, he displayed a knowledge of physics, albeit more than somewhat fragmented, that displayed a knowledge far beyond someone who was instructed only in Physics 101.

So, to recap, we have the Allende letters to Jessup as being the source of the research and investigation that sprouts the legend and literature regarding the Philadelphia Experiment. Jessup investigates matters and is also contacted by the Navy. He becomes disturbed at what he discovers and disappears before being found dead in Florida. Ivan Sanderson, Gray Barker, and others take up the cause and produce various articles and publications. Ultimately, William Moore and Charles Berlitz publish their book *The Philadelphia Experiment: Project Invisibility* which brings the subject to the mainstream. Of course, the story does not end there. Eventually, *The Philadelphia Experiment* is released as a motion picture and this unleashes a whole new chain of events. Preston Nichols, Duncan Cameron, and Al Bielek emerge and connect the time experiment in Philadelphia to that of Montauk, New York. Wild and preposterous stories are held together with hitherto unheard of technical explanations and approaches to the phenomena surrounding time. New avenues of thought are opened to the imagination.

When I come along and hear the stories of Preston, Duncan, and Al, I work with Preston in order to write the most cohesive account possible at the time. This results in the birth of an entirely new legend: The Montauk Project, a series of mind control and time experiments which allegedly connected to the 1943 version of the Philadelphia Experiment itself.

I find the predicament of Carlos Allende somewhat similar to Preston Nichols. Both were programmed or mind controlled and seem to "leak" information that comes from an unpredictable source and certainly flows in an unpredictable manner. However, Preston is much more together as a personality than Allende was and is also available for dialogue. He is also a scientific genius. Like Dr. Jessup, I also encounter strange coincidences or patterns of what we call "synchronicity." But, unlike Dr. Jessup, the coincidences I discover are not disturbing. I take these coincidences and use them like chess pieces to discover new facets and connections in an attempt to explain what is going on. A whole new genre of literature has thus been created which has turned into "The Montauk Saga," and the eternal quest to discover the secrets of time and the universe itself. This book, *The Philadelphia Experiment Murder: Parallel Universes and the Physics of Insanity*, which is based upon the murder of Phil Schneider, is an important piece of literature in this regard.

I have referred to the death of Phil Schneider as the second "Philadelphia Experiment Murder" because his life is inextricably connected to this incident and the quantum potential that it represents to all of humanity. In a bigger sense, the "Philadelphia Experiment Murder" also refers to efforts by some to literally "murder" the legend or story itself and thus cut off mankind's reach to an expanded reality and consciousness of itself. Most importantly, it should be recognized that Phil Schneider died as a martyr for the cause of truth. His life and efforts to expose the truth should never be forgotten.

Although I was personally very well aware of the outrageousness and implications of Phil's death, time and circumstances did not allow me to engage in a personal investigation of the matter. This responsibility was placed in the hands of Alexandra Bruce, a very capable researcher and writer who has more than a little acumen for this type of research. I first met Alexandra many years ago at a lecture in Manhattan. When she told me her surname, I inquired if she was aware of the particular nature of that name's Scottish heritage. I was, of course, referring to King Robert I "the Bruce." His army won independence for Scotland by defeating the English in the Battle of Bannockburn. Those of you who are familiar with my earlier work will remember that the Stewart family were the original guardians of the Stone of Scone and, by that reason, are the rightful heirs to the throne of the British Isles. The purpose of the Jacobite rebellion was to restore the Stewarts to that throne.

Looking further into Scottish history, I discovered that the legitimacy of the Stewart's clan's claim was due to Walter Stewart's marriage to Marjorie Bruce, daughter of Robert the Bruce. Walter had commanded the left wing of the Scots army at Bannockburn and had been knighted by Bruce on the battlefield. The son of Marjorie and Walter Stewart, Robert II ascended to the throne of Scotland after her brother, King David II died in 1371. The Scottish crown was thereby passed to the Stewart clan. Alexandra's uncle, Duncan Bruce, has been the North American representative for the chief of the Bruce clan, Lord Elgin, for over two decades.

A multi-cultural and multilingual individual, Alexandra attended Brown University after growing up in the United States and Brazil. At Brown, she was befriended by John F. Kennedy Jr. and was also a good friend of his wife, Carolyn Bessette. She grew up surrounded by the trappings of wealth, so-called "beautiful people," and with a distinguished pedigree. While this might sound either impressive or pretentious (depending on your viewpoint), Alexandra would be the first to tell you of the dark side of privilege. She has discovered how the mind-control tentacles of MK-ULTRA are a multigenerational labyrinth that reach into the most powerful families in the world as well as the celebrated and famous. Upon graduating from Brown, Alexandra founded her own film production company and became a leading producer of "rap" music videos in the early days of that musical genre. In addition to working in the film industry, she is a multi-talented individual who has experienced various adventures and misadventures. Currently, she works as an executive at a Long Island investment firm. *The Philadelphia Experiment Murder* is her first book, and I think you will find it a very good one that not only maintains the intrigue of past books of mine but opens up new territory. Of more importance is that it exposes the horrendous injustice of a murdered man and his efforts to expose the truth.

Peter Moon
December 2000

1

PHIL SCHNEIDER'S DEATH

On January 17, 1996, an officer from the local Clackamas County Sheriff's Department broke into Phil Schneider's apartment. He was accompanied by Al Pratt who had been leading regular Bible study groups with Phil and had come by Phil's apartment several days in a row. He had seen Phil's car in the driveway, but there had been no answer at the door.

Phil's bloated dead body had been in the warm apartment for about a week by the time it was discovered by these two men. The corpse was found in a most unusual position. The head was resting on the seat of a wheelchair and the rest of the body arched under an adjustable high-rise bed. Beneath the body and on the floor was a pool of blood. There was no blood on the wheelchair.

The initial cause of death was a judgment call by the police officer, Detective Randy Harris. He said there was no sign of a struggle and that there were no scratch marks. Harris determined that Phil had suffered from a stroke while seated on his bed, and that he had fallen face forward onto his wheelchair. He deduced that the pool of blood was from a brain hemorrhage which had spilled out of his mouth. What the detective failed to explain was how this stream of blood had missed the wheelchair which is exactly where Phil's head was resting when the body was found.

The apartment building's superintendent retrieved Phil Schneider's emergency card that was on file. The only name listed was that of Phil's friend, Blaine Schmeer. Not too long before Phil's death, Blaine had been set to inherit most of Phil's personal effects which consisted mostly of mineral samples. Just a few weeks earlier, the two close friends suffered a major argument and Phil had cut Blaine out of his will. Blaine arrived at the apartment and, upon viewing the body, thought that it was in an unusual position. Detective Randy Harris, however, did not think so and released the body to the Mount Scott Funeral Home.

This turned out to be the first of many irregularities by officials in the investigation of Phil Schneider's death. It was also a major irregularity that Phil's body was removed without a coroner or assistant coroner ever coming to the scene of the death. It is a violation of Oregon State law for a body to be removed from the scene of a death-at-home without the body first being examined by a coroner.

During many lectures he gave over the course of the previous two years, Phil Schneider often referred to constant attempts being made on his life. These ranged from staged "accidents" to running gunfights. Phil was quite well known on the patriot and UFO lecture circuit for speaking out about underground base activities. He said he would continue to talk until somebody succeeded in killing him. This is evidently what had finally happened.

Two days after Phil's body was found, an astonishing discovery was made by the mortician at the funeral parlor. When the body was removed from the body bag to be prepared for cremation, a rubber tube was discovered embedded in the inflated folds of Phil's decomposed neck. From the autopsy photos, it is hard to imagine how this evident murder weapon could have been overlooked. It was actually wrapped three times around his neck and was double knotted. Supposedly, this was missed earlier because the massive swelling of tissue had obscured the tubing at the scene of Phil's death. Refrigeration in the morgue reduced the swelling in the body and thus enabled the weapon of death to rise to the surface.

This failure to discover the implement that killed Phil until long after his body had been removed from the scene is a flagrant oversight that would not have occurred if it had been properly examined by a coroner, as dictated by state law. This should clearly have been a murder investigation from the start, and it deserves to be a murder investigation to this day.

The funeral director, Rob Gasgill, was fuming mad at the discovery of the apparent murder weapon on his premises. Covering up murders was not part of his job description. He went out of his way to store Phil's body free of charge for several days past the company policy while Phil's ex-wife, Cynthia Drayer, decided whether to bury his body for possible future exhumation or to have it cremated, a more affordable alternative to this single mother on a fixed income.

Rob Gasgill assured Cynthia that the Clackamas County coroner was very good and gave her his name and number. However, since the Mount Scott Funeral Home was located in neighboring Multnomah County, the autopsy was to be performed there by the local Medical Examiner, Dr. Karen Gunson. According to Cynthia, Karen Gunson's autopsy report had "so many discrepancies, that it almost felt like it was not the body of Philip."

21

These inconsistencies related to what Cynthia knew full well about the state of her ex-husband's beleaguered body. Gunson made no mention of Phil's plastic sternum, the metal plate in his head, his tracheotomy, and the fact that half his right lung had been removed. His genitalia were described as "unremarkable" in the report while Cynthia states that his penis was very remarkable, having been "sliced down the bottom, from tip to back, like a hot-dog bun," due to massive injuries and infection that Phil said he had incurred while working as a construction engineer in Vietnam. Gunson did, however, note a "roughly triangular red-brown abrasion which is horizontally oriented in the right upper arm measuring 2' x 1/4'."

The autopsy photos are definitely of Phil's body, very clearly showing a rubber tube wrapped three times around his neck and double knotted at his throat. Phil's housekeeper said that he had been very weak and in a lot of pain recently. He would strap the arms of his body brace to his bed to keep his arms from moving at night. In order to write, he needed to use a ball with a pen stuck in it. His left hand, missing three fingers, had already been eighty percent disabled for many years. Phil sometimes wore a specially-fitted rubber bag to collect his involuntary urinations due to poor bladder control. In fact, he was wearing this catheter device at the time of his death and similar rubber tubing is what was found around his neck. Dr. Gunson quickly declared the cause of death to be "strangulation by ligature asphyxiation," the manner of death a suicide. In other words, he had strangled himself to death with the rubber tube.

According to a twenty-year veteran New York City detective that I queried, this kind of self-asphyxiation is NOT humanly possible. Suicide by hanging, he said, is quite feasible and relatively common. Death by hanging involves using the weight of the body to block the intake of oxygen and it often results in breaking the neck, but this was not the case with Phil Schneider. Additionally, this detective told me that the pool of blood "didn't sound right" either. He said that once the heart stops pumping, blood does not exit the body unless a vein or artery has been cut, and this had not happened. Did that pool of blood actually belong to Phil? This was never ascertained.

From a legal standpoint, once a death is ruled a suicide (or natural causes, for that matter), the guidelines governing the further investigation of the case diverge dramatically from that of a murder or a potential murder. Examination of the circumstantial evidence, such as blood work, is not considered worthy of the taxpayers' money to pursue in the case of a suicide. This is understandable from a budgetary point of view although one can see how an invocation of "suicide" can be abused by an agenda that does not want the disclosure of certain facts.

Phil Schneider's ex-wife knew him too well to believe that he would ever commit suicide, let alone by such a bizarre (and impossible) means as self-strangulation. Though they were divorced, they were still close friends. He had strong religious convictions that forbade suicide. Despite the great physical difficulties and pain which he endured daily, he told her more than once that if cutting off his legs would give him another year to live, he would definitely do it. In the event that he were ever to be put on a life-support system, he said, "Don't pull the plug, you never know, I might come back!"

Phil and his friends and associates were excited about future projects. Mark Rufener, who had last seen Phil on January 7th, was in the process of buying land with him in Colorado. The two were scheduled to collaborate on a book about UFOs, aliens, the Black Budget, and the

One World Government. Phil had recently borrowed a gun from another friend for the stated purpose of protecting himself. He also had a variety of prescription painkillers that would have been more efficient for the task of committing suicide if that had been his real intention. Cynthia is positive that he was committed to living his life, watching their daughter grow up, and alerting the public to what he thought was really going on with U.S. taxpayers' Black Budget dollars.

The following is a direct quote from an email Cynthia sent to me:

"The body was taken to Mt. Scott Funeral Home (located in Portland, Oregon, Multnomah County), per my instructions to the sheriff that night after they called me. The next day I went to the funeral home and asked to view the body, and the funeral director, Mr. Gasgill, suggested that I not do that, because of the advanced state of decay and smell. I told him of my suspicions, and he told me how he trusted the coroner's office in Clackamas County. He did not realize at the time that no coroner had been out to view Philip's body...the director must have [then] gone in to view Philip's body, and was shocked to find a rubber hose wrapped around his neck.

"Mr. Gasgill was outraged at having been delivered a body that was 'compromised', and called the Portland sheriff's office who must have contacted the Clackamas sheriff's office. Rather than take the body all the way back to the Clackamas County coroner's office (which is 40 miles round trip), they simply took the body to the medical examiner's office near Eastmoreland Hospital in

Portland, Oregon, Multnomah County.

"I was later to find out that the Clackamas and Multnomah sheriff's office do not get along. I think at the point of the autopsy, the Clackamas County sheriff's office and coroner's office were trying to cover up their botched job...I called Dr. Gunson about a week after the autopsy and asked her to do drug analysis of the samples taken from Philip's body. Although I gave her reasons for my suspicions of foul play, she refused to have the samples analyzed but promised to keep the sample for one year instead of the normal three months.

"When eleven months had gone by, I arranged for an independent analysis of the samples and contacted Dr. Gunson to transfer the samples. THEY WERE MISSING. I had Philip's body cremated based on Dr. Gunson's promise to keep those samples a year and certainly felt betrayed by her incompetence. I have a lot of complaints, both toward the coroner's office of Clackamas County and the medical examiner's office in Multnomah County.

"Even though I sent a several page letter outlining why I felt that Philip had been murdered, I only received negative responses from the sheriff's office and coroner's office. They never reopened Philip's file and never ordered the necessary drug analysis of the samples from his autopsy. It turned out to be an $88.00 test, not the $2,000.00 test I was told by Dr. Gunson. If I had known that, I could have had the samples tested before the three-month time period. I'm fuming right now because the total injustice of this is just welling up in me.

"Philip didn't deserve to be murdered. My only hope is to have his story told by people like you."

Phil's brother, George Schneider, has long been and continues to be a sheriff in Multnomah county. He knows every cop in the Portland area and could have easily pushed for a more thorough investigation of his brother's death. On the contrary, he wrote a letter to Cynthia urging her to simply accept the fact that her ex-husband was dead.

Cynthia distinctly remembers a conversation that occurred during a Thanksgiving dinner when Phil brought up the subject of George having been a test pilot at Area 51.

Cynthia said, "George told Philip that he better stop talking about such things or he would end up dead. Really, that is what he said."

The oversights on the part of Clackamas and Multnomah Counties are glaring and point to a cover-up in the legal investigation of Phil Schneider's death. My investigation into this story thus far, which includes the perusal of hundreds of official documents furnished to me by his ex-wife, has led me to conclude that Phil Schneider did not kill himself. He was murdered. Who killed him and exactly why are unclear. It is my hope, as well as that of Cynthia and the rest of Phil's friends, that his case will one day be reopened so that justice can be obtained for his death.

2

WHO WAS PHIL SCHNEIDER?

Who was Phil Schneider and why would anybody want to kill him? During the two years preceding his death, he lectured extensively around the country about his involvement in the construction of secret government underground bases. The bases he claimed to work on included Area 51 in Nevada and the base at Dulce, New Mexico. Phil routinely told his audiences that he was breaking the law by discussing these projects and that he was in breach of his national security oath. Although he indicated there had been many attempts made on his life, Phil felt morally driven to talk about these things because, as he said, "I love my country more than I love my life."

Professionally, Phil Schneider was a geologist and an expert in the design of "shaped charge" explosions. This involved leading teams to drill holes a mile or so into the earth and taking core samples to detect areas of porous rock strata surrounded by harder rock. These are the optimal conditions for the controlled implosions in which they would blow huge underground spaces (sometimes as big as three cubic miles) into existence. Often, his teams would be linking preexisting cave systems.

Phil said that he worked on black budget projects for seventeen years. A copy of his filing for federal disability insurance in 1981 lists his employers between 1977 and 1981 as Morrison-Knudsen, a construction company contracting for the U.S. Department of Defense and later for the U.S. Overseas Projects Division. He worked directly for the Department of the Navy, Office of Naval Intelligence between August of 1978 and January of 1981. On the lecture circuit, he told audiences that when he quit his black budget job in disgust, he cut up his ID card and mailed it to his boss. This was the same year he began speaking publicly about black budget projects.

Phil had some bizarre things to say about what was happening with trillions of U.S. tax dollars. He alleged that an element of the government was in an uneasy collaboration with negative extraterrestrial groups. A faction of the military had been acquiring and developing alien technologies in exchange for human genetic material, but this alliance had unraveled into a war that was going on beneath our feet. He claimed to be one of three human survivors of a clash between sixty government employees and gray aliens in a legendary skirmish, long known to conspiracy buffs as the "Dulce War," which supposedly took place in an underground base in New Mexico in 1979.

On display at Phil's lectures were samples of alien metals he said he had acquired over the course of his work. Also on view were enlarged photographs of UFOs scooting past mushroom clouds at the 1946 Bikini Atoll nuclear blasts. Phil's father, Oscar Schneider, who served as a medical officer in the Navy for thirty years, had taken these photos.

Phil added that his father was a German U-boat captain who had been captured by the Allies and inducted into the U.S. Navy at the height of World War II. Much has been written about the CIA's Operation Paperclip, a sort of "Witness Protection Program" for Nazis in which German SS officers were given new identities and repatriated as United States citizens in the years following WW II. There are many tactical reasons why it would have been in the interest of national security to do this.

If it is true that Oscar Schneider was a captured Nazi, his story is all the more remarkable in that his repatriation would have occurred as early as 1941. Two official records of his that I have seen are typed onto bureaucratic Navy forms entitled "Officer Biography Sheet" and a "Statement of Personal History." Both refer to his 1906 birth in San Francisco and the destruction of his original birth certificate in the resulting fire. There is, however, a major discrepancy with the 1906 birth date in San Francisco.

Cynthia Drayer, while doing unrelated genealogical research, established that as of 1902, all California state birth records were automatically shipped to Sacramento. So, the story about Oscar's original birth records being burned in the post-quake fire is a lie. Additionally, the above-referenced documents conflict with two others that are apparently out there, each one stating Oscar Schneider's birthplace to be a different town in California. I will say more about this later.

What is known for sure is that the Germans in the 1940's were far more advanced than the Allies in their development of submarine technology. A captured German with high tech information of the kind possessed by Oscar Schneider might have been too valuable to the Allied effort to be left to rot away as a POW. While there is no irrefutable proof that Oscar was a captured Nazi, there is ample documentation of his involvement in the 1950's of the development of air circulation systems used

STATEMENT OF PERSONAL HISTORY

Above is a naval form entitled "Statement of Personal History" which indicates Oscar Schneider's birth records were destroyed in the fire of 1906, a statement which is highly suspect if not outright and intentionally false.

11.	DATES		FOREIGN TRAVEL (Other than as a direct result of United States military duties)		
FROM	TO	COUNTRY VISITED		PURPOSE OF TRAVEL	
None					

12.	MONTH AND YEAR		EMPLOYMENT (Account for all dates or periods)		
FROM	TO	NAME AND ADDRESS OF EMPLOYER	IMMEDIATE SUPERVISOR (Name)	REASON FOR LEAVING	
1925	1931	Part-time employment in a number of drug stores as Pharmacist in Portland, Oregon			
1931	Present	Medical Officer, U.S. Navy			

HAVE YOU EVER BEEN EMPLOYED BY A FOREIGN GOVERNMENT OR AGENCY? ☐ NO
HAVE YOU EVER BEEN REFUSED A BOND? ☐ NO
IF "YES," EXPLAIN (Use Item 19 for more space) SOCIAL SECURITY NO.

13. CREDIT AND CHARACTER (Give three business and five personal references, stating business address of all references if known. Do not include relatives, former employers, or persons living outside the United States or its Territories)

	NAME	YEARS KNOWN	STREET AND NUMBER	CITY	STATE
CREDIT	Woodward & Lothrop	12	Washington, D.C.		
	Willard Hotel	12	Washington, D.C.		
	Fidelity-Phila. Trust Co.	14	Phila., Pa.		
CHARACTER	Joseph Pettit, MD	26	610 S.W. Alder Street	Portland	Oregon
	V.Adm. Ross R. McIntire, MC, U.S. Navy (Ret)	12		Coronado	Calif.
	Capt R.S. Barnaby, USN (Ret)	14	2107 Chancellor Street	Philadelphia	Pa.
	Mr. Glen R. Hall	17	3511 Utah Street	San Diego	Calif.
	Mr. Walter A. Schneider			Camp Springs	Md.

14. RESIDENCES DURING PAST 15 YEARS (Do not include military stations)

	MONTH AND YEAR		STREET AND NUMBER	CITY	STATE OR COUNTRY
	FROM	TO			
1.	Oct.1940	Aug.1941	Harvard School of Public Health, 55 Shattuck Street	Boston	Mass.
2.	Aug.1941	Oct.1942	Harvard Hall Apts., Harvard Street,N.W., Washington,D.C.		
3.	Oct.1942	Feb.1943	No record of street address	Pensacola	Florida
4.	Feb.1943	Jan.1945	Middletown Apts., 148 East 48 Street	New York	N.Y.
5.	Feb.1945	Dec.1945	N.A.S. (occupied govt. quarters)	Brunswick	Me.
6.	Dec.1945	Jan.1946	N.A.S.	Banana River	Florida
7.	Feb.1946	May 1949	2810 28th Street N.W.	Washington, D.C.	
8.	Jun.1949	Sep.1950	3090 Buena Vista Way	Berkeley	Calif.
9.	Oct.1950	Sep.1952	1622 Argonne Place, N.W.	Washington,D.C.	
0.	Sep.1952	Jan.1955	3609 34th Street, N.W.	Washington,D.C.	
1.	Feb.1955	Present	Pelham Cottage, Pelham Street	London, S.W.7.	England

STATEMENT OF PERSONAL HISTORY

Above is page two of Oscar Schneider's Statement of Personal History from the Navy and indicates he lived in New York, a three hour drive from Philadelphia, during the time of the Philadelphia Experiment.

in nuclear submarines. There are also documents detailing his responsibility for monitoring the radiation effects of the Bikini Atoll nuclear tests on the crewmen involved. Both of these officer class positions were in extremely sensitive Cold War Navy projects.

The record shows that Oscar served with distinction during his three decades in the Navy. Early in his professional life, he helped formulate the first U.S. Navy Radiological Safety Regulations. These established the parameters for safe exposure levels to different kinds of radiation for the human body. He ended his career as the Chief of the Division of Biology and Medicine under the Secretary of Defense with "regulatory cognizance of all biological and medical research conducted by the Armed Forces," answering directly to the Joint Chiefs of Staff and retiring in 1961. Oscar Schneider was definitely no slouch.

During the period between 1943 to 1945, Oscar Schneider's resume states that he was the Senior Medical Officer on two aircraft carriers on the East Coast. His family was stationed in Pensacola, Florida and in New York City during those years. Interestingly enough, Oscar's official permanent address on all of his records during his thirty-year stint in the Navy was "Fidelity Philadelphia Trust Company, Philadelphia, Pennsylvania." If Oscar was originally from California, and if he was never stationed in Philadelphia, why was his official permanent address there?

The above data is particularly interesting due to Phil's claims, along with his supporting evidence, that Oscar Schneider was the Senior Medical Officer in charge of the infamous August 12, 1943 Philadelphia Experiment. There are several official photographs of Oscar aboard the *U.S.S. Eldridge*, the vessel said to have been used in the experiment. At his lectures, Phil distributed

IN REPLY REFER TO
NO. ....

1900 hours

U. S. NAVAL AIR STATION
PENSACOLA, FLORIDA

12 Dec., 1944.

In consideration of the latest facts in considering the fate of the U.S.S. Farnsworth - (DE-173); all ships personnel and material must be quarantined absolute until further notice, NO EXCEPTIONS. An on site Naval inspection is ordered forthwith, as Bureau of Ships reticent requirements in section 93-A. Please include DE-173's ships' log to Adm. Roscoe Hillenkoetter, USN. Consider them and all events of nature ABOVE SECRET, see clau. ARH-9 "Project Blue Sky".

OSCAR SCHNEIDER, CAPT., U.S.N.

LETTER OF DECEMBER 12, 1944

This letter is dated one year and four months after the Philadelphia Experiment took place and asks for a quarantine of all affected personnel. For a more in-depth analysis and a transcript of the above, see Chapter 4 of this book.

IN REPLY
REFER TO:

0545 hours

JOINT TASK FORCE ONE 17 April, 1953.

190 RHO
USAAF- Unit 9
Q L B - Section
Lt. Gen. NATHAN F. TWINING.

In proper perspective - the 'Philly'
Navy Yard's bungling of what should have
been a routine exhaustive search of the
U.SN. Vessel DE-173 shows total lack of
substance and detail in your department.

As of 0600, 21 April 1953, J. Edgar
Hoover now requests that all associated
personnel be given prior and restrictive
Psychological Testing conducted by the Navy
Psychological Unit at Quantico, Virginia.

Be it also forthwith that the U.S.
Army Intelligence 19 group be sent in to
assist any further snafus by U.S.N. and
related personnel.

O. Schneider Capt. USN.

PRIORITY   2-A   - STYX 190 RHC

LETTER OF APRIL 17, 1953

This letter is dated nearly ten years after the Philadelphia Experiment.
It suggests that all associated personnel have "prior and restrictive
psychological testing" at the naval facility in Quantico, VA. See
Chapter 4 of this book for a transcript and more details.

IN REPLY
REFER TO:

0145 *hours*

JOINT TASK FORCE ONE 23 April, 1953.

E. U. Condon:

Ed,

Please excuse our concern at USN hdqtrs over the "flap" concerning the TE-173. As you might now know, this affair has been on our collective minds for some near ten years. As for the subsequent escape of seven of its original crew from over Psychol. Unit in Virginia - be rest assured of their immediate capture as Hoover now considers such matters as sectional classification: 1-A PRIME DIRECTIVE.

As far as seeing your work at Colorado U. in Boulder, we plan to attend your lecture and study. Thank you for your concern of N. Tesla's "Spatial Analyzer" type device as now we have the 'gizmo' too!

Please send on Reno's work as to initiate new "Philly" naval workings of immediate future.

Respectfully,

CAPT., USN.

—PRIORITY 2-A

LETTER OF APRIL 23, 1953

This is dated six days after the previous letter and refers to the escape
of seven of the crew members from Quantico and to Nikola Tesla's
"spatial analyzer." See Chapter 4 for a transcript and more details.

DEPARTMENT OF THE NAVY
BUREAU OF MEDICINE AND SURGERY
WASHINGTON 25, D. C.

1400 hours
6 march 1955.
IN REPLY REFER TO

C. I. Farnborough's, M.D.
47 - RHYOLITE Section
ATIC - A-13 HTPP.

Charles,
    Conducted autopsy on #9 crew member of DE173 with some abnormal conclusions as to foreign material (perhaps implants) found in #9's cerebellum part 14-3. The subsequent analysis of the 1⅛" long gold tipped fiber shaped something like this:

[diagram of elongated fiber-shaped object with measurement 1⅛" length]

ENLARGED DETAIL:

[enlarged diagram] — unknown 'script' or 'writing'

    Can you identify using your analytical methods?
    Four of these mysterious devices were removed from #9 - DE-173's crew member; as nasal cavity also showed implantation.

C. [signature]
CAPT. U.S.N.

PRIORITY 2-A

LETTER OF MARCH 6, 1955

Written nearly two years after the previous two letters, this letter is addressed to another military surgeon. It refers to an autopsy of a crew member during which an implant was removed from his brain. See Chapter 4 for a transcript and more details.

four documents in Oscar's handwriting on official Navy letterhead relating to the Philadelphia Experiment. These papers are either remarkable forgeries or are the only official records of the project yet to have surfaced. Phil vowed that his father, Oscar, confessed to him on his deathbed about his involvement in the Philadelphia Experiment and told him the whereabouts of these documents. If they are fake, we must ponder why anybody would go to such lengths to fabricate a hoax of that nature.

Many readers of this book will be familiar with the story of the Philadelphia Experiment propounded by lecturer Al Bielek and others. They claim that it was a top secret radar invisibility (proto-Stealth) project conducted by the Navy during the height of World War II that had strange and unprecedented results. On the U.S. Navy's Internet website, there is a whole section devoted to denying that this experiment ever took place. As "proof," the logs of the *Eldridge* are supplied for the months of September and October. But, what of its whereabouts on August 12, the date of the fateful experiment? The vessel was not officially commissioned until September. This made it the perfect venue for top secret tests of the kind the self-professed survivors allege took place in July and August. The following is a brief recap of the highlights of the story for those who are not familiar with it.

During the early part of WW II, radar was still cutting edge technology and the U.S. was desperate to have an advantage over the Germans who, at that time, were on the verge of winning the war. The U.S. Navy tapped the top brains of the world to manipulate the unified field energies in order to cloak a destroyer escort, the *U.S.S. Eldridge,* from radar. The scientists purported to have been involved were Nikola Tesla, inventor of the alternating current generator; John von Neumann, inventor of the modern computer; and a host of Princeton University physicists. Known by its participants as Project Rainbow, a series of tests were conducted over the course of approximately one month. The initial tests were done in the Brooklyn Naval Yard with later ones in the Philadelphia Naval Yard. This is where the unexpected events of the August 12th test gave the project notoriety as the "Philadelphia Experiment."

Essentially, they generated an enormously powerful electromagnetic field, mostly in the range of radio waves, around the ship. This intense field was powered by harnessing the vast amount of telluric "free energy" emanating out of the Earth itself. This energy field is referred to as the "geomagnetic grid" as it manifests itself in intersecting lines around the Earth. Called "ley lines" by students of European megalithic sites, these bands of magnetic energy were also known as "dragon paths" by the ancient Chinese. Tesla fans believe that harnessing and distributing this free energy was his chief goal in life and conspiratologists theorize that Tesla was murdered by the petroleum cartel that did not want knowledge of this free energy to become commonplace.

I use the term "unified field" here to refer to the mathematical understanding of the quantum interplay between the frequencies of the entire electromagnetic spectrum: light, sound, radio waves, gravity, time, etc. These forces are all interrelated with one another and together, along with the component of consciousness, form the fabric of space-time. These could also be called "the forces of Creation" as they create the constructs of reality as we know it.

There are also those who say that Tesla and the Princeton-Navy team had achieved a measure of control over space-time physics and that Project Rainbow was

U.S.S. ELDRIDGE

Above is a photo of the *U.S.S. Eldridge*, the destroyer escort upon which the Philadelphia Experiment was allegedly conducted. The ship was eventually sold to the Greek Navy along with some of its sister ships. It has been reported by people in Greece that the names of the ships have been shifted around to confuse the issue of which ship is which. The *Eldridge* was reportedly scrapped, but no one can be sure it was the actual *Eldridge* and not one of the sister ships.

actually a test to teleport the *Eldridge*. According to this scenario, the ultimate objective of the project was to perfect their ability to teleport materiel and troops to anywhere on the Earth's geomagnetic grid at any time.

As the legend goes, the *Eldridge* did not merely disappear off the radar screen nor merely from plain sight. It disappeared from this reality entirely — for about twenty minutes. While gone from the Philadelphia Naval harbor, the *Eldridge* was sighted in many diverse places. Different accounts had it appearing like some kind of giant quantum particle off the coast of Norfolk, Virginia; somewhere in Northern Italy; in the Gobi desert; and off of Montauk Point, New York. When the *Eldridge* finally reappeared in Philadelphia, several men were dead and some were found melded into the steel of the ship. Some were "phasing" in and out of view while others were spontaneously combusting. The rest were either driven insane or at least sounded insane from what they reported about their foray into hyperspace.

According to Phil Schneider, it was the job of his father, Oscar, as the chief Medical Officer of the Philadelphia Experiment, to autopsy the sailor's bodies and assess the effects of the massive electromagnetic fields on the survivors. Among the documents that Phil displayed to support this were the previously mentioned four official letters handwritten by Oscar on Navy letterhead.

There will be a more in-depth discussion about these documents later, but one of these letters includes a drawing and description of an "implant" Oscar removed from a sailor's body, a 1 1/8" long fiber with a conical-shaped gold tip on which there was an indecipherable script. This document lends support to Al Bielek's theory that the Philadelphia Experiment was an alien manipulation all along which enabled beings from another space-time continuum to invade our reality. This supposedly paved the way for the thousands of worldwide UFO "flaps" and reports of alien abduction in the ensuing decades.

The gist of Phil Schneider's information is that the lives of he and his father were deeply embedded in the military's secret involvement with interdimensional "alien" intelligence. From the videotapes and transcripts of his lectures, as well as from the affirmations of Cynthia Drayer, it is clear that Phil Schneider was genuine in his mission to alert the public to what he believed to be a vile encroachment on human freedom.

Whatever their relative truth, his claims were difficult to verify. They were a total assault on the prevailing "conventional-consensus" reality. But, Phil was hardly alone in the kind of claims he made. His statements have found corroboration in the firsthand accounts of other self-professed high security defense contractor employees, military personnel, and "alien abductees."

Phil was not a skilled public speaker, but he emanated an unvarnished sincerity that was compellingly heartfelt. With the indignation of an insider, he would constantly refer to the machinations of the impending "New World Order" although he never gave an explanation of exactly who and what the NWO was. He was not particularly good at deliberating intricate political plots. He was a nuts-and-bolts type of guy who had the personality of an engineer. His lectures focused on the esoteric technologies that were being used by the "Secret Government" and withheld from the public. He was absolutely fascinated by stealth technology, mineralogy, and the different molecular structures that metals could take on under different gravitational conditions from those of Earth. On the blackboard, he would draw up and compare his own Time Variance Formula with that of Nikola Tesla and show his audience how the formula explicated the ability of UFOs to exceed the speed of light.

It was when Phil would describe his experiences of physical combat with grey aliens that any hope of his story going mainstream went out the window. His credibility deficit from discussing such things was further complicated by a tendency to contradict himself in the details of his stories.

Whatever the truth is about Phil's details, the fact remains that scores of people worldwide have reported abduction experiences where they were taken to underground bases and observed U.S. military servicemen working side by side with aliens. There are also other people claiming to be ex-government employees whose stories of back-engineering alien technology and other details mirror Phil Schneider's claims. Regardless of whether their reports can be physically proven, there does seem to be an alien reality that a mass of people are directly experiencing on some level of their being. The earnest sincerity of Phil's speaking, with its strange ring of truth, begs for a deeper look into his story.

3

THE TRUTH

Phil Schneider's wife of two years, Cynthia Drayer, says "Philip could do upper level mathematics but could not fill out a doctor's form." She also states that his mood swings were frequent and intense and that he would rapidly switch from one state of being to another. Physically, he could be very powerful and had registered "lethal hands" according to Al Bielek. Despite this, he might be confined to a wheelchair by the end of a day. Although never officially diagnosed with Multiple Personality Disorder, Phil displayed the characteristics of this condition. Cynthia attributes his disjointed behavior to brainwashing he underwent following his high security employment.

Phil Schneider's outrageous and sometimes contradictory statements wreaked havoc on his credibility. One researcher, who had initially set out to defend Phil's claims, eventually concluded that he was mentally ill and posted this deduction worldwide on the Internet. This judgment had been bolstered by the researcher's conversations with Phil's own brother who told him that Phil was a self-mutilator who had chopped off his fingers with a hacksaw and lived off government disability checks his entire adult life.

This state of affairs has served to prevent a better understanding of Phil's life and a proper investigation of his death. Was Phil Schneider a troubled crank who fulfilled his paranoid hallucinations of being stalked by the "Secret Government" by taking his own life? Or was he, in fact, murdered by agents of the government because he had violated his national security oath and because his seemingly wild claims contained classified information?

As Phil's apparently incomprehensible conduct can be more properly understood with an understanding of the technology of heavy-duty mind control and the population groups to which it is applied, it is worthwhile to digress from Phil's story for a moment and have a look at this topic.

More and more cases of brainwashing or "debriefing" are beginning to emerge in conjunction with UFO episodes involving the military. A prime example of this occurred with witnesses of the 1981 Bentwaters Air Force Base case in England. This is a joint British-U.S. base where a UFO is said to have landed in front of several servicemen. Some of the American soldiers reported that they were taken to a section of the base underground where they were drugged and hypnotized after witnessing UFOs land on the base.

Peter Robbins, author of *Left at East Gate*, an extremely well-documented account of the case, has told me he believes that part of what the soldiers remembered about the whole affair was actually a psychological warfare setpiece staged in an underground facility they were taken to after being heavily drugged. Their superiors, dressed up with rubber alien masks, acted out a bizarre scenario that would never make sense if they ever tried to explain it to anybody. The unwitting soldiers were used as guinea pigs in a test of what they could be made to believe they had seen and heard because the actual truth about what happened to them was considered so crucial to security that it absolutely could not come out. This is called a "screen memory" where one bad memory is used to screen another one.

If it is true that Phil Schneider worked on black budget underground projects for seventeen years, it is likely that he was brainwashed on several occasions. This, in turn, would indicate that, at least part of the time, he was unknowingly spewing disinformational programming.

If it is true, as suggested by his brother, that Phil Schneider was a self-mutilator, this could actually be a clue that lends a degree of credibility to Phil's claims of involvement in high security underground bases. It may also shed some light on his seeming inability to keep his stories straight as a severe compulsion to self-mutilate is a very common symptom of people suffering from Dissociative Identity Disorder (also known as Multiple Personality Disorder).

Dissociative Identity Disorder is the typical human response to extreme ongoing trauma. The ego/personality "splits off" and creates alternate personalities in order to contain and isolate the profoundly traumatic memories from the "base" personality. DID is the condition that is systematically induced in the subjects of the most savage form of brainwashing: trauma-based mind control.

Since employees of high security operations are routinely "debriefed" as a matter of security, a discussion of Phil Schneider, underground bases, and/or aliens is grievously incomplete without a word about mind control. Research on mind control, spanning several decades, has been conducted by the CIA and U.S. military and is a matter of public record as shown by many documents obtained through the Freedom Of Information Act. These documents, some of which are posted all over the Internet, show the official start of the mind control Project MK-ULTRA to have been in 1953. Additionally, official documentation is available on similar projects as early as the mid-1940's.

There are many well-researched books and monographs on Project MK-ULTRA and its 140 or more subprojects in print and on the Internet by several authors. Notable works include those of Jonathan Marks, Alexander Constantine, Colin Ross, Katharina Wilson and Martin Cannon, the latter persuasively arguing that "alien abductions" are actually screen memories relating to secret mind control experiments that have nothing to do with actual aliens whatsoever. It is interesting to note that Cannon has since denied this position. Was he coerced or otherwise brainwashed to retract himself?

Although there is far more official documentation and proof of secret government mind control experiments, this subject is immensely more taboo than the so-called "alien abduction phenomenon" which, interestingly enough, has been gaining an increasing level of acceptance in the mass media as a bonafide experience.

There is nothing new about mind control. It is as old as the human race and its drive for control. The manifold aspects of mind control, information control, and their degrees of intensity are as varied as consciousness itself. They range from advertising and "spin control" to the darkest and most depraved manipulations of the human mind imaginable.

Extensive knowledge about the nature of the human mind and the means of controlling it has been accumulated by certain secret societies over the millennia. The initiatic cults of the ancient world made powerful observations about the effects of ritual and the near death experience on the human psyche. The assassin cults of the Near East embellished upon these effects with the use of drugs and hypnosis. These techniques were acquired by the Templars who brought the knowledge back to Europe during the Crusades. This body of esoteric information was honed by the Catholic Church, especially during the Inquisition, when the mind-shattering effects of physical torture were explored. All of the above was improved upon by the Nazis and the CIA in the latter half of the 20th century.

In the process of trauma-based mind control, a person is first completely broken down psychologically. After that, he is then built back up to the specifications of the controller. It is recounted that hundreds, if not thousands, of personality fragments can be systematically created in a human being with each personality or "file" programmable with information and skills that can be triggered by various means and of which the "base" personality is blissfully unaware. Different combinations of drugs, hypnosis, "stimuceiver" brain implants, electromagnetic and optophotonic brainwave entrainment devices are also reportedly used to control an individual's thoughts and actions. The worker/agent can thereby be allowed to roam freely in the world without compromising the security of an operation.

These are the protocols that are rumored to be among those used to create "ultimate warriors" such as Navy Seals and other Special Forces operatives and combatants. The creation of such subjects is reported to be an aspect of the Monarch Project, a subproject of MK-ULTRA. The following is an excerpt from an article entitled "Project Monarch: Nazi Mind Control" by Ron Patton and published in the Fall 1996 issue of *Paranoia* magazine:

"The most incriminating statement to date made by a government official as to the possible existence of Project Monarch was extracted by Anton Chaitkin, a writer for the publication, *The New Federalist.* When former CIA Director William Colby was asked directly, 'What about Monarch?' he replied angrily and ambiguously, 'We stopped that between the late 1960's and the early 1970's.' "

It is interesting to note that Colby was eventually found dead floating in Chesapeake Bay under mysterious circumstances. Continuing to quote from the above-cited article:

"Dr. Corydon Hammond, a Psychologist from the University of Utah, delivered a stunning lecture entitled "Hypnosis in MPD: Ritual Abuse" at the Fourth Annual Eastern Regional Conference on Abuse and Multiple Personality, June 25, 1992 in Alexandria, Virginia. He essentially confirmed the suspicions of the attentive crowd of mental health professionals, wherein a certain percentage of their clients had undergone mind control programming in an intensively systematic manner. Hammond alluded to the Nazi connection, military and CIA mind control research, Greek letter and color programming and specifically mentioned the "Monarch Project" in relation to a form of operative conditioning. [These Greek letter codes for programming levels include:]

ALPHA: Regarded as 'general' or regular programming within the base control personality; characterized by extremely pronounced memory retention, along with substantially increased physical strength and visual acuity. Alpha programming is accomplished through deliberately subdividing the victim's personality which, in essence, causes a left brain-right brain division, allowing for a programmed union of L and R through neuron pathway stimulation.

BETA: Referred to as 'sexual' programming. This programming eliminates all learned moral convictions and stimulates the primitive sexual instinct, devoid of inhibitions.

DELTA: This is known as 'killer' programming, originally developed for training special agents or elite soldiers (i.e. Delta Force, First Earth Battalion, Mossad, etc.) in covert operations. Optimal adrenal output and controlled aggression is evident. Subjects are devoid of fear; very systematic in carrying out their assignment. Self-destruct or suicide instructions are layered in at this level.

THETA: Considered to be the 'psychic' programming. Bloodliners (those coming from multigenerational satanic families) were determined to exhibit a greater propensity for having telepathic abilities than did non-bloodliners. Due to its evident limitations, however, various forms of electronic mind control systems were developed and introduced, namely, biomedical human telemetry devices (brain implants), directed-energy lasers using microwaves and/or electromagnetism. It is reported these are used in conjunction with highly-advanced computers and sophisticated satellite tracking systems.

OMEGA: A 'self-destruct' form of programming, also known as 'Code Green.' The corresponding behaviors include suicidal tendencies and/or self-mutilation. This program is generally activated when the victim/survivor begins therapy or interrogation and too much memory is being recovered.

GAMMA: Another form of system protection is through 'deception' programming, which elicits misinformation and misdirection. This level is intertwined with demonology and tends to regenerate itself at a later time if inappropriately deactivated."

Some of the most sophisticated mind control protocols involve the embedding of disinformational programming and layer upon layer of false cover stories in the subjects' memories. When subjects begin to break their programming by delving into their past involvement in high security posts or experiments, bizarre "memories" often come to the surface. No matter how earnest and honest they are, the hapless subjects cannot distinguish between their real memories and those that were programmed. Likewise, the hapless investigator gets stuck in a quagmire surrounded by a hall of mirrors. It is very devilish.

For example, Phil's stories about working side-by-side with "big-nosed Greys" can be taken at face value by the credulous or taken to be programmed screen memories by the more suspicious. The skeptic can walk away from the whole thing by pronouncing all of the above to be insane. The hard-core conspiratologist, surmising that Phil suffered from induced insanity in the form of Dissociative Identity Disorder via high tech mind control, agrees to an extent with the skeptic. Something for everyone, folks. It's a "keep 'em guessing" game, and it works.

Although I have never seen any documentation of this, I suspect that Top Gun-type fighter pilot training might involve heavy programming as well. You're not going to hand over the keys to a $20 million aircraft to some kid unless you are pretty sure of how the pilot is going to perform. An interesting story relating to this comes from Peter Moon who, while doing some research, went to the neighborhood where Jack Parsons, inventor of the solid fuel rocket and cofounder of the Jet Propulsion Laboratory, lived and worked in Pasadena, California. On the street, he bumped into a WW II RAF pilot. When Peter asked him if he knew anything about the great rocket scientist, the old timer motioned to a nearby building and said: "Everything you want to know about went on in that building." When Peter asked him what he meant, the Englishman very eerily replied: "Implants! Implants! Aviation implants!"

Brain implants are not the stuff of science fiction. They are a reality. There are numerous patents for various kinds of brain implants, and several models are currently being used in mainstream medicine. These include cochlear implants for the hearing impaired and neural stimulators to control the artificial limbs of amputees.

Even if only a small fraction of the above-described mind control scenarios are true, it is a horrendous proposition. Such is the resilience of the human life-force, however, that many people who report having been thusly manipulated have managed to derive positive and empowering insights about their own lives and about consciousness itself. Others have not been so lucky.

One can readily assume that there are underground bases in existence to provide secure locations for the development of the latest defense technologies and to serve as housing for a ruling elite in a "worst case scenario" such as a nuclear holocaust. Even if there is no such thing as a joint military/"big-nosed Grey" base, these facilities are of the very highest security.

It would therefore stand to reason that maintaining the invulnerability of such immensely secret installations would require that the personnel submit to certain protocols beyond the taking of an oath. After all, these employees would have access to highly sensitive information by merely being at the locations at all. The deployment of any or all of the latest technological breakthroughs in hypnosis, pharmaceuticals, electronics and good old trauma to guarantee the successful encryption of a person's high security memories is understandable from the point of view of the interests of "national security."

What could be a more effective means of maintaining precious security without actually physically imprisoning personnel? I do not know what the actual statistics are on the productivity of the Nazi and Soviet forced labor camps, but I would be willing to bet that the output ratio of any fine U.S. defense contractor today is more efficient although they are notorious for being just the opposite. Having been programmed to "remember to forget" any beans they had to spill, high-clearance employees/operatives who suffer brainwashing would never think of spilling the beans.

This principle works well on paper and in the field until there is an unexpected break in the programming. An illustrative example of a case of this is Duncan Cameron, the famed "time-traveler" of the Montauk series. Prior to his deprogramming, he thought that he had spent the last twelve years of his life as a "Bayman," one of an old breed of Long Islanders who scoop oysters and clams off the floors of the local bays from their tiny skiffs. Being that he was groomed for wealth and privilege as a product of exclusive boarding schools, this career path did not make a lot of sense. What emerged in his deprogramming process was that he had been drafted by the NSA after his tour of duty in Vietnam to be used in what was probably the most high security series of operations in history, the Montauk Projects. The "Bayman" identity was a convenient cover because it is a solitary profession and the area where it is practiced is nearby the Montauk base.

It is not inconceivable that the assertion that Phil was a self-mutilating loser who lived strictly off of disability checks was based on a screen memory implanted in the mind of his brother. Remember, there is ample documentation that their father, Oscar Schneider, was involved in some extremely high security projects during his thirty years as a naval officer. In this line of reckoning, it becomes more plausible that there was some truth to what Phil Schneider had to say and the discrepancies in his stories finally begin to make some sense.

4

THE DOCUMENTS

I have in my possession a copy of Phil Schneider's filing for Social Security Disability payments. Included in the list of his employers from 1974 through 1981 are Morrison-Knudsen, Inc. as a U.S. Department of Defense construction contractor and the Office of Naval Intelligence, Overseas Projects Division. I also have a copy of a photograph of an approximately eight year old Phil and his two siblings on the White House lawn for an Easter egg hunt. This does indeed suggest that his father was a VIP in government circles.

Aside from the above, the most persuasive hard evidence available to back his stories is a stack of his father's Navy documents and photographs which Phil found in his father's basement after the latter's death. Most of the papers were of the standard bureaucratic variety relating to prosaic matters such as expense reports and Oscar Schneider's health examinations. However, among these documents were four intriguing memos, apparently written and signed by Oscar in longhand on Navy letterhead, referring to the Philadelphia Experiment. These are reproduced in Chapter Two. The following versions are translated from the cursive writing.

Analysis of Document #1: This letter is dated 12 December 1944, exactly one year and four months after the Philadelphia Experiment took place. The letterhead is that of the U.S. Naval Air Station in Pensacola, Florida. This does not entirely correlate with other Navy documents I have. One, a "Statement of Personal History," lists his residence between October 1942 – February 1943 as Pensacola, Florida, "with no record of street address." Between February 1943 and January 1945 his street address is listed as 148 E. 48th Street, New York, New York. This would place him in New York City, only three hours or so away from the Philadelphia Naval Yard at the time of the Philadelphia Experiment. At the time this memo was written, he was still residing in New York, yet the letterhead says Pensacola. Oscar had been stationed there but not for two years; however, military personnel often shuttle between different locations and assignments. When they are involved in high security operations, the paper trail can be all the more confusing to researchers.

Another "Officer Biography Sheet" I have lists Oscar's "Ship-Unit-Station" as the "*CVE Block Island*, Senior Medical Officer" between February 1943 and September 1943 and the "*CV Hornet*, Senior Medical Officer" between October 1943 and January 1945. It appears that he was officially aboard those ships while his family lived at the Florida and New York residences.

The *U.S.S. Faruseth* mentioned and incorrectly spelled in the document refers to a civilian vessel docked at the Philadelphia Navy Yard at the time of the invisibility experiment. DE-173 refers to the number of the *U.S.S. Eldridge*, the destroyer escort used in the experiment. It was from the *Faruseth* that, legend has it, Carlos Allende witnessed the Philadelphia Experiment. Allende was the person credited for "breaking" the Philadelphia Experiment story in a series of 1956 letters to ufologist and scientist Morris K. Jessup. Jessup was later found "suicided" in his car while researching the Philadelphia Experiment. His death is actually the first "Philadelphia Experiment Murder" and spurned researchers to dig further into the mysterious enigma that still begs for more official answers.

IN REPLY REFER TO   1900 HOURS

No................................   12 Dec,, 1944

U.S. NAVAL AIR STATION
PENSACOLA, FLORIDA

In consideration of the latest facts in considering the fate of the U.S.S. Farunseth – (DE-173); all ships personnel and materiel must be quarantined <u>absolute</u> until further notice, NO EXCEPTIONS. An on site Naval inspection is ordered forthwith, as Bureau of Ships reticent requirements in Section 93-A. Please include DE-173 ship's log to Adm. Roscoe Hillenkotter, U.S.N. Consider these and all events of nature ABOVE SECRET, see class. ARH-9 "Project Blue Sky."

OSCAR SCHNEIDER, CAPT., U.S.N.

Document #2: This letter is dated 17 April, 1953 and nearly ten years after the Philadelphia Experiment. It suggests that the ramifications of the apparent slipshod follow-up of the Philadelphia Experiment were still being felt in Oscar's department. This resulted in FBI chief, J. Edgar Hoover, ordering all associated personnel to have "prior and restrictive psychological testing" at the naval facility in Quantico, VA. This reads like an order to debrief and/or brainwash all of the surviving participants. In addition, a special unit of Army Intelligence was being sent in to supervise this injunction. Ironically, the date of the "psychological testing" coincides with the advent of MK-ULTRA.

JOINT TASK FORCE ONE

0545 hours

IN REPLY   17 April, 1953
REFER TO:

190 RHO
USAF – Unit 9
GLB – Section
Lt. GEN. NATHAN F. TWINING

In proper perspective – the "Philly" Navy Yard's bungling of what should have been a routine exhaustive search of the U.S.N. Vessel DE-173 shows total lack of substance and detail in your department.

As of 0600, 21 April 1953, J. Edgar Hoover now requests that all associated personnel be given prior and restrictive Psychological Testing conducted by the Navy Psychological Unit at Quantico, Virginia.

Be it also forthwith that the U.S. Army Intelligence 19 group be sent in to assist any further snafus by U.S.N. and related personnel.

O. Schneider Capt. U.S.N.

PRIORITY   2-a   STYX 190 RHO

Document #3: This is dated six days after the previous letter and refers to the escape of seven of the crew members from the psychological testing facility in Quantico. Oscar assures the addressee, "Ed Condon," of their capture as the whole affair was recently classified as "1-A Prime Directive." The letter also refers to Tesla's "spatial analyzer" and suggests that his department is continuing to plan "Philly-type" experiments.

JOINT TASK FORCE ONE

0145 hours
IN REPLY   23 April, 1953
REFER TO:

E.U. Condon:

Ed,

Please excuse our concern at U.S.N. hdqtrs over the "flap" concerning the DE-173. As you might now know this affair has been on our collective minds for some near ten years. As for the subsequent escape of seven of its original crew from our Psychol. Unit in Virginia – be rest assured of their immediate capture as Hoover now considers such matters as sectional classification: 1-A PRIME DIRECTIVE.

As far as seeing your work at Colorado U. In Boulder, we plan to attend your lecture and study. Thank you for your concern of N. Tesla's "Spatial Analyzer" type device as now we have the 'gizmo' too!

Please send on Reno's work as to initiate new "Philly" naval workings of immediate future.

Respectfully,

O. Schneider
CAPT., U.S.N.

PRIORITY 2-A

Document #4: Dated March of 1955 and nearly two years after the previous two letters, this letter is addressed to another military surgeon. It refers to an autopsy of "#9 crew member" during which a 1 1/8" gold-tipped implant with "unknown script or writing" on it was removed from his brain. Oscar is asking if this doctor can identify the writing using his "analytical methods."

Detractors have already suggested that Phil forged the above letters on the Navy stationery he had available through his father. Having viewed handwritten documents by both Phil and Oscar, I have to say that Phil's handwriting could never be confused with the longhand on these documents. A 1990 sample of Oscar Schneider's handwriting looks like the same handwriting of the memos except that it was by that time addled with arthritis. I have noticed a slight difference in the "S" of the signature on the "Philly" papers versus two other signatures I have by Oscar. It is possible that it could have varied slightly over the years.

Although I am not experienced in handwriting analysis or graphology, I did have the opportunity to have the documents examined by two individuals who are. See Chapter 5.

DEPARTMENT OF THE NAVY
BUREAU OF MEDICINE AND SURGERY
WASHINGTON, D.C.

1400 hours

SEAL OF THE   6 March 1955
DEPARTMENT OF DEFENSE

IN REPLY REFER TO:

C.I. Farnsborough, M.D.
47- RHYOLITE SECTION
ATIC – A – 13 HTPP.

Charles,
Conducted autopsy on #9 crew member of DE-173 with some abnormal conclusions as to foreign material (perhaps implants) found in #9's cerebellum part 14-3. The subsequent analysis of the 1 1/8" long gold tipped fiber shaped something like this:

DRAWING OF IMPLANT
ENLARGED DETAIL:
ANOTHER DRAWING

Unknown 'script' or 'writing'

Can you identify using your analytical methods?
Four of these mysterious devices were removed from # 9 – DE-173 crew member; as nasal cavity also showed implantation.

O. Schneider
CAPT. U.S.N.

PRIORITY 2-A RHO – RNY

5

HANDWRITING ANALYSIS

The following is an analysis of the Oscar Schneider documents by an individual who does not want to be named because his regular profession frowns on speculative work. Additionally, he does not guarantee any degree of accuracy. It is as follows.

"First of all, I'm not commenting on the rather spectacular and somewhat questionable content. Neither am I commenting on the style and suitability of the grammar and word selection, that to me is also suspect. I'm confining my comments to the handwriting style itself. This is believed by some to yield clues to the personality of the writer, and the mood they were in when it was written.

The writer is fairly emotionally expressive, but not overly so, about normal for that generation. (Subsequent generations are showing less emotional expression.) The writer shows a good balance between the ethereal and the concrete. The writer is not overly optimistic or pessimistic. There are some tendencies for both self-deception and deception toward others, however they are not overpowering, and can be a self-protection or protected mode of communication. They do not indicate outright lying. The signature shows a healthy ego. The last page shows the writing of an older person. I can't tell if it is the same person or not. There are some similarities and some differences. To me, it is inconclusive."

Besides giving me the above analysis, this graphologist was kind enough to forward a sample of the handwriting in these documents to his mentor who also wishes to remain anonymous. The mentor learned the art from his father who taught the subject in years past. The following is what the mentor had to say about it.

"The writer looks as if he was told to write this. The writer will not let the reader "into" his head. This is the tip of the iceberg, the writer knows more than he is telling. He is not making this up. He is good at keeping quiet. He is not an entrepreneur, he is a cog in a wheel. He is not an originator. Not a con man. He knows what he is doing. On page four: He is definitely directed. He does not work alone. There is no greed or no ulterior motive. He does not volunteer information.

"On page five: Possibly the same person a good ways down the road. Similarities but cannot definitely say it is the same person. This writer shows an increased level of bitterness, but also more relief. Not as fully together as the earlier samples, more loose ends. The writer is domineering, and has developed a "cranky" attitude. We use the term "he" for the writer, but handwriting analysis cannot identify gender."

While the preceding neither proves nor disproves the validity of the documents, it does provide some insights into the person who wrote them. It all supports the scenario of an intelligence operation of some sort and that there is much more to the entire story than the author of the documents will ever let be known.

6

THE NAZI CONNECTION

Phil's friend, Al Bielek, who is the main surviving proponent of Oscar Schneider's secret history, believes the aforesaid documents are genuine. In his lectures about the Philadelphia Experiment, Bielek regularly shows slides of official Navy photographs of Oscar Schneider aboard a vessel that is believed to be the *U.S.S. Eldridge.* The following is an excerpt of an interview I had with him:

Bruce: As far as Cynthia knows, Oscar Schneider was an American born in Portland or somewhere in the Northwest, but you know another version of his story.

Bielek: The official Navy record says Oscar was born in Chico, California in 1905. I read the official record when Phil still had it. All of Phil's papers disappeared after his death. Oscar went to the University of California at Berkeley and then to Harvard Medical School to get his medical degree. He enlisted in the Navy, became a medical doctor and went up to the rank of Captain. That's the official version.

Bruce: That's different from a Navy document that Cynthia sent me a copy of, a "Statement of Personal History," which referred to his birth in San Francisco in 1906 and the destruction of his original birth certificate in the fire resulting from the great earthquake of that year. [This same document also states that Oscar Schneider's father, Philip Schneider, was born in Russia, "about 1867", naturalized as a U.S. citizen "around 1890" and that his mother, Gerta Melzer, was born in Poland "about 1876."]

Bielek: Well then, that makes three different versions. I've seen another version that the Navy put out that says Oscar was born in San Jose, California in 1906. So, there's three versions and none of them are right. His real history, which he told to Phil when he knew he was dying, in the last two weeks of his life...and he wouldn't let his brother sit in on it because he didn't like him...he told him, "Everything you know or have heard about me is false. I originally came from Germany. I was a master machinist at the age of fourteen."

Now, to become a master machinist, as I understand it, requires that you pass a very rigorous test. You start from raw material, like a block of metal and cut it and machine it and do all the things necessary to produce a finished product without any assistance or any ready made materials or parts. So, it's extremely difficult to become a master machinist and, needless to say, he did this all by the age of fourteen, so he was evidently very gifted.

Somewhere down the line, he joined the German Navy and wound up being a U-boat captain.

In '38 or '39, I'm not sure when, he actually was rated as a Captain of a U-boat. He went around the planet sinking enemy ships, enemies of Germany, of course...Allied ships. This is before the Americans were in the war. A total of sixty-eight ships he sank, I believe.

Bruce: So, Oscar told all of this to Phil on his deathbed?

Bielek: That's right. Oscar told him all this before he died. Oscar carried with him, as did all U-boat captains, gold bars with which they could negotiate for all they needed. All the gold bars had the "das ein skullen," the skull and cross-bones, on them as well as another Nazi stamp.

He was captured by the French in 1940 and brought into a French court. There were negotiations ongoing and he was turned over to the Third Army. And then, for some reason, the negotiations going on have him turned over to the United States Navy. That's how they transferred him. They brought him in in late 1940, early '41, and the same night he was to be terminated, they put him in the U.S. Navy's Medical Corps.

Now, Phil doesn't know where Oscar got his knowledge of medicine, but apparently, his knowledge was sufficient to pass the MSD. And, he was in charge of all medical aspects of the Philadelphia Experiment. I have a lot of documentation of that in particular.

Bruce: I've seen copies of those documents, but I wonder why, if they were official memos written

71

by Oscar to other officers — and Cynthia says she's seen the original envelopes with the postmarks — if he had sent these memos, what were they still doing in his possession?

Bielek: I really don't know why they were. She didn't have the originals. Apparently, Phil destroyed the originals and made a bunch of copies. Something about the National Security Act and possible espionage charges if he had the originals. That was the reason she believed that Phil had destroyed the originals. So, he circulated the copies — you've seen them — and they've been around quite a bit.

So, he [Oscar] was in the Navy and nobody really knows exactly why or how he got in the Navy in view of the fact that he had apparently been in the German Navy. But, he was there. We got pictures of him on board the *Eldridge*, pictures of him at his office in the Pentagon, and all the copies of his correspondence.

And, as he said to Phil, "You know, I was involved in the Philadelphia Experiment program for eight years and so many things went wrong, you haven't a clue! I got absolutely tired and fed up with it and I didn't want to know what went on with it anymore. So, I transferred out and became part of the nuclear sub program under Rickhold in 1957." I have pictures of him aboard the first nuclear submarine.

Bruce: Apparently, he designed something on it... the air circulation system?

**FINAL BRIEFING ABOARD THE *USS ELDRIDGE*
9 AUGUST 1943**

The above photograph was discovered in Oscar Schneider's
basement after his death. The man in front with the blonde hair
and prominent chin has been identified as either Don or Val Thor.
Val Thor is featured in the book *Stranger in the Pentagon*, but the
character in that book looks quite different. The character above
has been identified as his brother Don. Both are allegedly aliens
who have major influence at the Pentagon. The man directly in
back of "Mr. Thor" is Oscar Schneider. He has a crewcut
and is wearing an overcoat while clasping his hands.

Bielek: The air circulation and air conditioning system. And, he stayed in the Navy until he retired.

Bruce: Now, that is something that is never supposed to happen — that a foreigner can even be aboard a nuclear submarine.

Bielek: They had to do a lot of record manipulation. That's why they came up with the so-called "certified history" of where he was born, when and so forth...which would make him an American rather than a German. But, when you look at him, he's obviously Teutonic in origin.

Bruce: So, he was not Jewish?

Bielek: No, he was not Jewish. He was German.

Bruce: So, that was another part of his false identity?

Bielek: That's correct.

Bruce: That was a big psychodrama in Phil's family. His mother, Sally's family, apparently disowned her for having married a Jew.

Bielek: Well, part of what he told Phil before he died was "I'm not Jewish." Being Jewish was part of his cover history. There's no way that he would have gotten where he did in the German Navy if he were.

Bruce: I wouldn't think so!

DOES THIS MAN LOOK JEWISH TO YOU?

This is Oscar Schneider seated at a desk while in the U.S. Navy. Although he was officially Jewish, he was not a religious person but was reported to be a repatriated Nazi who served as a senior medical officer. He was also an expert in submarine technology.

OSCAR "OTTO" SCHNEIDER

This is Oscar Schneider in naval dress uniform. On his deathbed, he confessed to his son that he worked as a Nazi U-boat captain before his capture by the French. The U.S. salvaged his career by giving him a commision in the Navy as a Captain where he worked as a doctor and reportedly montitored the crew of the *U.S.S. Eldridge*.

Bielek: I haven't thought of this in a while, but there was a documentary done some years ago; put out by PBS and WGBH in Boston entitled "Codebreakers," a very interesting story about how they broke the codes of the Japanese and so forth in WW II. At the tail end of the story, it shows a picture of a German submarine that was captured by the French. The captain of the ship is on the deck surrounded by his sailors and the resemblance to Oscar is very striking.

Bruce: Really?

Bielek: Yes. It's not too good of a shot because it was taken off some old 16mm footage that was somewhat deteriorated before it was transferred to video. I want to have it enhanced, but I would swear that it was him. They made no mention of the captain or the ship or anything else. They just stuck this thing at the end of the documentary; for what reason, I don't really know.

Bruce: Interesting.

Bielek: There is some, SOME supportive evidence that Oscar Schneider really was in the German Navy insofar as the gold bars were concerned. Phil said he had them. They were in the vault, the safety deposit box. His father gave them to him. When I went up to Portland after his death, nobody knew where the gold bars were.

Bruce: Cynthia told me about them. Phil had them analyzed and they were found to have dental alloys in them and fragments of teeth.

Bielek: I hadn't heard about that, but it's very possible. Very possible.

Bruce: She told me that Phil sold them, but he felt that, morally, he couldn't keep all of the money from their sale. He couldn't have that on his conscience.

Bielek: Well, I had heard that he'd sold them, but he hadn't sold them all. I never got the full story on that. But, he also had a huge gem collection, and I had seen some of that; and, of course, the huge rock collection which was still there in his apartment. But, the gem collection...he asked me on the phone if I could try and sell it for him, and I said, "Sure, give me a list," and I never got the list, but he told me later that he had sold it for $90,000. This $90,000 disappeared; was never seen again. He allegedly kept it in his apartment but, of course, you know what happened to his apartment [after his death].

Phil had some disagreements with a couple of people that included an entire group up there in Portland. He used to speak regularly before the Bigfoot Society. He gave lectures. I met them after his death. They told me he had some gold bars and that he had some people that he didn't get along with that included his own brother.

His brother, allegedly, has some of the missing records. I don't know. After Phil died, apparently, there was a book manuscript which disappeared. He tried to get it published in September of '95.

Bruce: Do you think that Oscar Schneider was his real name?

Bielek: Oscar Schneider was his real name, yes.

Bruce: "Otto" seems to be the name that people who believe he was a German officer refer to him as.

Bielek: Otto was his middle name. He was Oscar Otto Schneider. His correspondence was signed sometimes with both names; sometimes, he didn't.

Even if only a small part of the data from Al Bielek is true, Oscar Schneider is an obvious candidate for being a repatriated Nazi. Al's comments were corroborated by an email I received from Phil's ex-wife, Cynthia Drayer. Interestingly, although Oscar Schneider was nominally Jewish and this particular fact had caused turmoil in his wife's family, there was no evidence of any practice of Jewish faith. In response to my questions about Phil's religious background, she said the following.

"I don't believe (Phil) ever went through any of the normal "training" such as a Barmitzvah. He was Presbyterian while we were married and was associating with the Jehovah's Witness religion when he died. I never saw Oscar in any "Jewish" ceremonies. I never saw him celebrate any holiday except the Christian ones, like Christmas. They did not celebrate Passover or Chanukah."

With regard to Oscar's birth certificate, Cynthia had this to say.

"Although Oscar was born in 1906, I don't believe that his birth record would have been destroyed by the San Francisco fire. The reason for this is that all birth records were sent to the state capital (Sacramento) after 1902. The only reason I know this is because Leo, my first husband, was also born in San Francisco (small world, isn't it?) and his birth certificate WAS destroyed in the fire. He was born in 1890! At the time of Leo's birth, the records were kept at the county courthouse which burnt down right after the quake. The only way Leo could prove his citizenship and age for social security was using the 1900 census and his baptismal record."

Her comments on the gold bars were also compelling.

"About the Gold Bars - Philip became aware of the 'gold bars' after Oscar died and he went through the safety deposit boxes with his brother. Photographs were taken of the gold bars, and Philip stated that they had markings on them which made him believe that they were from the Nazis. I'm assuming that he had some excuse about 'authenticating' their worth and took some 'scrapings' off of one of the gold bars. I know for a fact that he had friends at the Columbia Coin Shop in downtown Portland, and he may have had the gold analyzed there. When he came to me about the bars, he was really 'worried' and morally concerned. The tests came back with 'dental gold traces' and microscopic teeth fragments, alloys and items that would not be in regular gold bullion. He discussed with me how he did not want any financial gain from them and would not take them from the estate; that his brother and sister could get the money from their sale. He did not want to profit from them at all. He never took any of them and never took any money from their sale. After Philip died, Oscar's estate was still being divided. I had the unpleasant task of dividing in thirds the rest of the jewelry and items from the safety deposit boxes for his daughter Marie, his only beneficiary. There were no gold bars at that time."

The irregularity of Oscar's birth records and the stories of the gold bars are intriguing and convincing to a certain degree, but they are not meant to be construed as absolute proof that Oscar was a repatriated "captured" German Officer. Being in possession of Nazi gold bars does not necessitate that one actually be of German birth. However, how he might have come into possession of such items by other means raises possible scenarios that are equally bizarre.

There is plenty of documentation to convince me that Oscar was involved in many high security activities such as the Bikini Atoll Nuclear tests, the Philadelphia Experiment and nuclear propulsion systems on submarines. There is a transcript of a lecture he gave on nuclear physics in 1951 and photographs of him surrounded by his shipmates and maps of the Bikini Atoll in the hold of a vessel. There are also photos of him aboard a ship identified as the *Eldridge* plus written documentation to support that he was involved in the above projects as well as many others of an equally sensitive nature.

It is absolutely clear that whoever exactly Oscar Schneider really was, he was quite valuable to the Navy. They invested a lot of time and money in training him in various skills throughout the years and his career of service appears to have been outstanding.

7

UNDERGROUND

Phil Schneider's ex-wife tells me that she is increasingly convinced that he was murdered because of the details he was revealing about secret government underground bases. For a good while, he had been speaking publicly about their exact locations, sizes, as well as each one's specific characteristics and main activities.

It is very difficult to verify claims of such a classified nature. Moreover, it is not the intention of this work to prove that everything Phil said was true. The fact of his father's involvement in several top secret Navy projects and the fact that Phil was strangled to death do lend a degree of credibility to what he was saying.

The exploration of the topic of underground bases immediately lands one in a topsy-turvy world where what is generally considered to be science fiction and fantasy is called the truth. One of the most grounded and well-researched books currently available about the subject of underground bases was written by Richard Sauder, Ph.D., entitled *Underground Bases and Tunnels: What is the Government Trying to Hide?* Interestingly enough, Sauder, who has no claims of clandestine involvement at these locations and who portrays himself as anything but a "crackpot," was prodded into researching his book by a singularly unusual circumstance. The following is a quote excerpted from an article he wrote for the March/April 1996 issue of the British *UFO Magazine*:

> "Over the Christmas Holidays in 1992, I was suddenly awakened one night from a sound sleep. As it happened, I did not have long to wait at all to find out why I had awakened. It seems that someone had an important message to deliver to me, by a rather unorthodox method. All of a sudden, I heard a voice speaking very clearly in my right ear. The voice said: 'The underground bases are real.' At this point, believe you me, I was all ears. It continued on for 2 or 3 minutes, telling me in general terms that there are secret underground bases; that there are people who live and work underground in the facilities; that the general public little suspect the existence of the secret facilities; and that if the public did know what went on underground, they would be astonished. The voice spoke like this for a few minutes and then stopped as abruptly as it began."

The world of underground bases is strange enough to make even a staid Ph.D. hear voices. Likewise, the Phil Schneider stories are way up there in the ranks of "High Strangeness." As with many other accounts of the underground, we hear of high speed levitating train systems, ancient Atlantean cities, and several alien races living underground for thousands or millions of years.

Al Bielek is the keeper of the Phil Schneider mythos and claims to have worked in underground bases himself. Since Phil was presumably killed because of what he was talking about, I feel that it is important to let Al recount what Phil told him about his work and let him tell of his own experiences in the underground. The conversation begins with a question by me asking him about "Rhyolite" with reference to the aforementioned Oscar Schneider memo of 6 March 1955.

Bruce: I'm seeing "Rhyolite" at the top of that page which is what Phil would say was his Security Clearance classification. What is "Rhyolite 38?"

Bielek: Let me show you Phil's statement here. It says: "Seventeen years in Black Projects, carried a Level 3 Security Clearance, Rhyolite 38."
When I was on a radio program with...who was the former FBI man out of Las Vegas at that time? Actually, he worked out of Dallas...

Bruce: Ted Gunderson?

Bielek: Ted Gunderson. I was supposed to be on all week. Then it was clipped back to two days. Then, clipped back to one day — two hours, really. Halfway through this program, I mentioned that Phil had a very high level clearance: Rhyolite 38. Somebody comes onto the program and Ted says, "Oh, yes, so-and-so." He knew him really well. This guy starts arguing with me about clearances. He says, "I've been in the NSA," and he says, "I know all the clearances that there are and there's no such thing as a Rhyolite 38 clearance." I said, "Oh, really? Well, Phil Schneider had it." He says, "There is no such clearance." And, I said, "Well, I know that there was, and he had it. It was a part of his unity and his clearance techniques. He had the clearance level such that when he went into certain facilities, he had to have an eyeball scan, hand scan, and, of course, his badge or card that he carried around. And the guy says, "That's all true. That is one of the systems that they use for very high level clearance, but there is no such thing as Rhyolite." And I say, "Well, and of course, you're going to tell me that there is no Black Card clearance either." He refused to answer the question and we were cut off the air.

Bruce: Really? Because Ted Gunderson is supposed to be a government insider who claims to be coming forward and letting the people know what's really going on!

Bielek: Yes, but...

Hunt: (Preston Hunt is in the room and hearing our conversation and briefly joins in.) Black Card clearance?

Bielek: Yes.

Hunt: That's above the President, right?

Bielek: Basically, it is. He knew things that the President didn't know. We're talking about Phil. Projects he was in...he told me the projects he was in. He spent months at Area 51. He was supposedly known as an interpreter for a guest of the government, a reptilian. And, he was all over Europe and became a part of NATO. He was a geologist for

NATO. He was in Russia. He was everywhere. He knew about the underground Russian subway systems that are like or identical to what we have. We have them here in the U.S. I've ridden on them.

Bruce: This is the thing where you put your hand on it and it powers it up? (I was referring to legends I had heard of ancient Atlantean subway system that is powered by "vril," the willpower and/or frequency of certain individuals which the equipment recognizes and lets them use. By merely placing one's hand on a panel, the magnetic subway train levitates and moves forward).

Bielek: No. The ones I was on were of a different system. It's two hours from California to New York. It's faster than a plane.

Bruce: So, where did you get on and get off?

Bielek: Got on in one of the downtown office buildings in LA and got off, in my case, got off at Montauk. There's a major interchange at Newark, New Jersey. East Coast Terminus Interchange and the entrance to that is through the ITT office building in downtown Newark. That much I remember.

Hunt: Really? And, you can't get into there unless you have clearance, right?

Bielek: Oh, you don't get in there unless you have the clearance code for the day, the month, or however they're doing it for that particular time period. You punch it in on the elevator, a special punch key panel, and you punch in the right code. Or, you have the card and swipe the slot and the elevator will go down below the basement level, straight down to where the terminal is. Typically, they're half a mile to one mile down.

Hunt: And this is —

Bielek: This is all over the U.S. and it goes into Canada.

Bruce: It's a levitating magnetic train.

Bielek: Yes, it's a magnetic drive. So, anyway, I just pulled this sheet about Phil Schneider the other day to make a copy. It says he was a Level 3. In the current coding system for clearances, Level 3 is not the highest there is. Level 3 is above Top Secret but there is up to a level 5.

Bruce: So, Rhyolite would be the...

Bielek: Rhyolite is a specific subdivision for the geologists. Rhyolite is a gemstone and, consequently, that was the labeling for the geologists. That particular clearance level involved geology, projects in geology, underground construction, and so forth. He worked on helping to build the underground rooms which literally were much larger than rooms. They were anywhere from one eighth to 3 cubic miles of underground space.

Bruce: And, Phil said that there were at least two

of these facilities in every state, if not more.

Bielek: He said that there were 131, and he was going to put out the locations of every one of them. He said it was all in the hands of friends of his in case anything happened to him because he knew it was going to sooner or later. There had been thirteen attempts on his life which were unsuccessful. They got him on the fourteenth. They changed the venue. They drew his friends in. People he considered friends were used to do him in. The other attempts were unknown people in various different services. They tried to run him off the road with a van; shoot at him. He got in an actual running gunfight with a guy and this sort of thing. The thirteenth attempt involved sawing the lugnuts of his wheels three quarters of the way off his car's axles. He flipped the car, hit the guard rail; it held together and he got out. The police came by and said, "What the hell's going on here?" He told them the wheel flew off his car and they found it and told him, "You must have some real nice friends out there. This wheel has been sabotaged." Phil had it fixed and continued to drive it. It was one of the old Tauruses — very tough cars. That was the thirteenth attempt that failed; almost got him. The fourteenth, involving friends...perhaps his ex-wife told you the story...I'm not sure if she did.

Bruce: I don't think so.

Bielek: She didn't? Oh, I told her what I thought happened, and months later, she came back to me on the phone and said, "Al, I think your version is about right," and I said, "What do you mean?" and she said, "My mother is very psychic." She said her mother went into a state one day and asked to be shown what had actually happened to Phil on the night when he died. And she was shown what had happened.

As I suspected, that night on the 10th, he went out at around 10:00 or 10:30 in the evening to the "76," his favorite diner which was 22 miles from his house. He liked to go out and get a very late meal. He met some people there that he knew. They weren't necessarily good friends, but he knew them, and they got into a wild argument that ended up getting louder and louder and finally, Phil said, "We don't want to continue this here. Let's go outside." So, they went outside to continue this, and they wanted to have a private discussion, not in the parking lot. Phil had a key to a local gravel pit where he used to go all the time looking for gems. So, they all go down there. He unlocks the gate. There are three other people besides himself, and one of them was his own nurse according to the story that was given. An interesting part of this is that Phil had lethal hands. They were registered as lethal hands. He could kill with his bare hands.

Bruce: Even though he was missing half the fingers from his left hand?

Bielek: He was very strong. He could kill a person with one blow, literally. He was trained. He knew how to do it. He told a story about how, one time, he was up in the mountains hiking with friends of

90

his when they were confronted by six unknown people in black uniforms with guns who asked them who they were and what they were doing there. He said, "I think the question is the other way around. "Who are you and what are you doing here? We have a legal right to be here." It got nasty and Phil managed to get all their weapons away from them. One of them had a laser gun — a bulky pack with a cable going to a thing with a lens on the end of it. I said, "Phil, you should have taken that thing," and he said, "Well, I didn't want to take it. I figured it was government equipment." It was some kind of strange laser device.

Bruce: Phil had several major injuries throughout his body.

Bielek: Yes.

Bruce: He would change his stories from time to time as to the origins of his injuries which leads me to believe that he was heavily heavily brainwashed.

Bielek: Well, I believe that he was at various times because of the fact that he was involved in certain very high security Black Ops.

Bruce: Wouldn't that just be the case for anyone who would be working in an underground base?

Bielek: It is. Yes, it's the protocol. When you leave, when you finish the project, they give you a "debriefing." This is a polite way of saying you're brainwashed. But it came back to him. He wasn't totally brainwashed because up until the point where he quit the service, he had full memory, essentially, of what he had done. When he left, he told me the story. He had been in NATO for about two years. He was in the Geologists Corps, and he was scheduled to be promoted to the head of his department of geology in NATO with a salary of $500,000 a year and, in three years, a retirement at $1 million a year. He already was making $200,000 a year as a government geologist. He said that he never served in the military, but he worked with the military a lot. He was a civilian, a direct government employee. He said that when he was in the NATO business, when he traveled in Europe and traveled in Russia, he had full access to Russia.

Bruce: He also worked on the construction of an underground base in New Guinea and fathered a child with a local woman there. That's what Cynthia told me.

Bielek: That, I never knew.

Bruce: His brother claims that he was a self-mutilator; that he sawed his three fingers off when he was a teenager with a hacksaw. But then again, someone who's been mind controlled is suffering from Multiple Personality Disorder and self-mutilation is a very common symptom of MPD.

Bielek: Phil claimed that it was an accident that happened in shop years before.

Bruce: Is it possible that his brother was involved

in Black Projects as well? I mean...the father was. His brother is quoted all over the Internet debunking Phil's stories.

Bielek: If he's in Black Ops, he's in one of the groups for disinformation. I met him once or twice, and I was not well impressed with him. I do not consider him an honest person. Phil apparently lost his fingers in two different accidents. He was in NATO. In Russia, he was in the underground subway system. He said theirs traveled at Mach 2.

Bruce: I have a speech of Phil's on videotape where he claims that he lost his fingers due to a cobalt radiation gun in the 1979 Dulce skirmish; shot by a seven foot tall big-nosed grey.

Bielek: He was involved in a lot of skirmishes in the underground before the one at Dulce. His main job was to bore holes down through the earth (from one to three miles) to check the rock structure down there to find out if it was suited for the construction of an underground base. He had become the expert on this. It had to be a certain type of rock, certain type of structure and so forth, to make shaped charges to blow the room into existence by collapsing porous rock. He said that, several times, they'd be drilling and the drill bit would hit air. They'd struck a cavern.

One time, he was in an underground section. He had to bring his own light and the air was very foul. There was a lot of dust, but he thought he saw something moving and realized that he was looking straight at a tall alien. He said he didn't know who was more shocked, the alien or him? Phil had a gun which he legally wasn't supposed to carry, but he grabbed it and shot the alien dead. The alien had been reaching for his weapon. Phil said that they die just like any human would only this wasn't human. He said, one time, it was a reptilian and another time it was a tall grey. There was more than one incident like this. He said he got burned by more than one of those radiation guns like the one from the Dulce fight. I've heard many accounts of that story. Sixty-four went in and four came out, and he was one of the four. He was carried out. He had severe burns when he came out. He said his guts were out on the cot. It cut his ribs; cut his chest open. We now have weapons comparable to the aliens' but, at that particular time, it was a nasty nasty fight.

Bruce: So, what would you say is the purpose of all of these hundreds of underground bases? What's the idea?

Bielek: That's a very good question. I have my own idea of what they're for. They're building a lot of our super weapons systems underground. They have a complete transportation-highway system where trucks can go across the country between military bases. It is a complete underground network of bases and cities including ancient cities that have been there for thousands of years, and it's all there in preparation for a potential invasion. Phil knew about all of it. He was the official interpreter for a reptilian at

Area 51. He went down there on business. He went down there periodically. A particular time, he went to the underground where he was supposed to go to and there was a Marine there who tells him, "The man you want to see isn't ready, he's busy. Have a seat here. When he's ready, we'll call you. Oh, yes, and look straight ahead. Don't look to the side." Of course, when you say that to Phil, he'll deliberately look to the side. He saw a smoky glass window panel and somebody on the other side. He saw what it was and it wasn't human. So, he made note of this. And after about half an hour, the officer he was there to see...I think he mentioned he was a general. I'm not sure now. They discussed their business, and after their business was over, Phil asked him, "Who's that, there behind the panel?" and he said, "Oh, you saw him? That's one of the guests of the government. We've been trying to get him to talk for quite some time," and Phil says, "Let me try," and the general says, "Well, everybody else has. There's no reason why you can't!" So, he had to be put into a special spacesuit-type structure with his own air supply and refrigeration system and external communication apparatus before he went to the room where the reptilian was. The temperature was 123 degrees Fahrenheit. The atmosphere was not normal: 18% argon and a lot of other things I don't remember.

So, he's sitting there trying to talk with it, and it wouldn't say anything. Finally, after an hour, this thing started emitting these strange squeaking sounds. With the denser atmosphere, the sound travels differently. So, if they do have a lower voice in a normal atmosphere, it may be more elevated in the atmosphere he was in. After a while, he got to understand what this guy was saying. He was talking in English, but it was hard to understand what he was saying because they can talk any language. They know all the languages basically. So, he got to understand what the guy was saying and told the general, who said, "Good. You're going to be here a while." He stayed there for three months as the official interpreter. I said, "What did he tell you? What was the conversation about?" Phil would never tell me. That was one of the few things he refused to tell me about.

Bruce: Did Phil ever tell you about exactly how he got started in this kind of work?

Bielek: Sure. He started in the "Skunkworks" in California working on the SR-71. He showed me a photo of himself with the SR-71, but it's not public. It was his own private photo. And, there's a later photo of him standing in front of one of the early Stealth fighters, not the B-2, in an Air Force jumpsuit. He said he actually flew in one of the early ones. He wasn't a pilot but, he worked with them and then he graduated. He somehow went from Burbank to working with Lockheed in geology. He never did state the whole story other than to say that he was self-trained.

Bruce: So, it didn't seem to be directly related to his father's involvement in this sort of thing.

Bielek: No. He did spend time aboard Navy submarines and some of the other military ships, but his father told him a lot about the Philadelphia Experiment. He didn't tell him everything, and I wanted to get to talk with his father while he was still alive because I was aware of what was going on. He was in and out of hospitals and nursing homes, and he was not well. He had cancer for years...finally succumbed to cancer. Phil had cancer, too. He had MS, cancer, and arthritis.

Bruce: Yeah. It's hard to believe he could kill anyone with his bare hands. He could hardly stand up. Cynthia said that he would, by sheer force of will, manage to pull himself together physically, spend the day with his daughter, and go to the mall or whatever. Then, he would collapse into his wheelchair at the end of the day. He was wheelchair-bound, but somehow, with the power of his mind, he'd be able to get out and walk around during the day.

Bielek: Yes. He was in a wheelchair when I first met him...an electric wheelchair to get around. I got him started on the lecture circuit. I got him sponsored for the lecture in Idaho in May of '95. We did some other talks all over the place, and he stopped using the wheelchair. He had a bladder problem. He had to carry around a catheter and this sort of thing.

Bruce: But even that was also not all the time.

Bielek: It wasn't an every day event. He'd take it with him as backup in case it got bad. His mind was very strong. He got over many of his problems..

All of the above reveals beyond the shadow of any doubt that Phil Schneider had incredible physical and mental challenges to deal with in his daily life. As are many of the others who have been involved with the abusive ends of so-called secret-government projects, he was a "survivor" until his brutal murder. He managed pretty well when you consider the enormous obstacles he had to overcome

The fact that Phil was murdered is a no-brainer. Exactly why he was murdered and by whom leads to enormously complex and intangible questions. Based upon his employment history and qualifications, it should not make anyone blink to realize that he was privy to a secret underground military culture that dealt not only with the defense of the United States but with the phenomena, whether true or based on mass hypnosis, that is known as "aliens."

The premise of this book is that Phil Schneider was murdered to cover-up information directly related to the enigma known as the "Philadelphia Experiment." Phil's father was ostensibly connected to that experiment and its continued research which is now known as either the Phoenix Project or the Montauk Project and/or all of the various offshoots.

The original "Philadelphia Experiment Murder" actually refers to Dr. Morris K. Jessup, the astrophysicist who was dead found in his car as an apparent result of carbon-monoxide poisoning. Like Phil Schneider, Jessup's death was ruled a suicide despite evidence to the contrary. It has been said that the outrage of this action led people to not only believe but to further investigate the phenomena regarding the Philadelphia Experiment. Since that time, there have been numerous attempts to silence any information on the subject. This lack of information is further compounded by deliberate disinformation entered by various parties to distract people from the truth.

The expose of the so-called Montauk Project by Preston Nichols suffers many of the same problems. Here we have a scientific genius who is plagued by memories of being programmed. His most recent work, *The Music of Time*, was censored and diluted by himself at the last minute because he feared repercussions from the political arena. Despite the fact that names were deleted and the sting was taken out of the book, there was a major attempt to stop Preston from promoting the work. On August 12th, 2000, Preston was traveling on the William Floyd Parkway on Long Island en route to Cablevision where he was scheduled to do four television shows for a cable-access program hosted by Janet Russell. Stopped by a police car, he was taken to an unfamiliar precinct where he was beaten twenty to thirty times with a nightstick covered with towels. Two officers were present. One told him not to appear on the show. Using towels in such a manner prevents any evidence by way of bruises. This was meant as a method of intimidation. Further investigation revealed that although it was a Suffolk County police car, the two individuals involved were not Suffolk County policemen. They were operating on their own. The particular car in question was reportedly checked out on that day to officers from another municipality whose job is to enforce safety and zoning codes.

The above is symptomatic of people involved in breaking the news on so-called secret-government projects. Hard evidence is discouraged, and we are left to put together fragments as if we were working with a jigsaw puzzle. A very interesting piece of the Philadelphia Experiment/Montauk Project puzzle appeared right after the death of Phil Schneider.

8

THE PRUITT CONNECTION

As Peter Moon put together the manuscript for
Montauk Revisited, he says that he was repeatedly frus-
trated by attempts to verify the information offered by
Preston Nichols. Although there are many tangible points
of corroboration, much of the "proof" has come in the way
of confirmation in terms of synchronicity. While this
should not be discounted and has a value of its own, it is
a different order of data than what a hard core document
researcher would want. Peter wanted this information as
much as anyone else, but it has proven very hard to come
by. However, he was struck by the fact that during their
private conversations, Preston Nichols made many off-
handed and casual remarks about his boss at Montauk.
The man's name was Jack Pruitt. He was identified in the
Montauk story as the man who held a gun to Preston's
head on that fateful day of August 12, 1983 when he
ordered Preston to sever the wires to the Montauk trans-
mitter. Not only did Preston remember him, but Duncan
Cameron and Al Bielek remembered him as well. There
was definite agreement on the man's identity. Peter
thought it would be very interesting if he could track this
man down and ask a few questions. Although he asked

Preston about his whereabouts, the man had long since moved and appeared untraceable. One day, at a lecture in Sacramento, Preston met a Montauk boy who said he knew Jack Pruitt and that he had ended up as psychiatrist in Sausalito, California. Preston informed Peter. A search was done, but Jack Pruitt could not be found. Although Peter met another man who remembered Jack Pruitt, this line of research hit a dead end. No traceable evidence could be found of Jack Pruitt, let alone his alleged connection to Montauk. That was until, one day, in 1996.

Peter had travelled to the Suffolk County Historical Society specifically to do some digging and find out what he could about the history of Montauk. Although he did not find what he expected there, he discovered a major clue when he broke for lunch and went to a health food store in Riverhead. There, he met Ariel Phoenix and they became very fast friends. Since that time, she has taken on the role of "Montauk Artist" and has done the cover for this particular book. As they spoke, she mentioned a gentleman she knew by the name of Glen Pruitt. When she offhandedly mentioned that his father had been involved in strange projects, Peter remembered the last name very well. He wanted to know if Glen's father was named Jack. Sure enough, it was!

Peter soon arranged for a meeting to take place between Glen, Preston, and Al Bielek. When Glen showed them pictures, there was no doubt in their mind. That was the Jack Pruitt they knew from Montauk.

It turned out that Glen had more than a considerable amount of acumen for this type of information himself. He was quite cooperative in addressing the situation. Interestingly, I already knew Glen myself as I had attended one of his lectures. Peter asked me to try and break ground with Jack and see if we could make any headway in verifying the Montauk Project. I knew we would have to be careful and discrete and plotted out a strategy with Glen.

At the time, Glen knew little about the Montauk Project and it did not hold much interest for him. He had read the Sky Books publication by that title only because of that story's relationship to the Philadelphia Experiment. Glen had grown up hearing a lot about the Philadelphia Experiment from his grandfather, Lee Pruitt. Lee told many stories to his grandson about his internship under Nikola Tesla while he was a student at the University of Colorado. He was very proud to say that it was he who had discovered the correct alloy from which to make the filaments for the specialized vacuum tubes that were used in the Philadelphia Experiment.

Before the invention of the transistor, vacuum tubes were used for the amplification of radio waves and other electromagnetic signals. In the Philadelphia Experiment, vacuum tubes were used to amplify the counterrotating electromagnetic fields that were generated around the *Eldridge* to cloak it from radar. The problem with vacuum tubes was that they tended to overheat. Lee recounted to his grandson that Tesla had sketched on a pad the shape of the molecule for a filament that would conduct the required current with a minimum of overheating. As Tesla's metallurgist, Lee was able to concoct the alloy that Telsa had visualized. Lee kept a couple of these old vacuum tubes in his office as souvenirs. We will discuss more of Lee Pruitt later.

When Glen agreed to meet with Preston Nichols and Al Bielek, he brought with him a group picture of the seventy-odd people employed at his father's insurance agency in 1983. As soon as Preston and Al immediately identified Jack Pruitt from the photograph, they proceeded to provide Glen with sufficient information to assure him that they did know his father. They said that he was the same Jack Pruitt who had issued their paychecks at Montauk though he seemed to look a bit older in the photo than they remembered. Glen told them that 1983 had been a rough year for Jack as his daughter had just been killed in a hit and run accident.

The declarations of Preston and Al came as a shock to Glen. They knew surprising details about his father "that they shouldn't have been able to know," but Glen still did not think their claims about Jack's involvement in the Montauk Project could be true. His reaction was, "They were nuts, but there must be some truth there."

As far as he knew, his father had always worked in Dallas, Texas. Until 1967, Carl Jack Pruitt was employed by Republic National Bank and then with Mutual of New York which is today the third largest insurance company in the world. Prior to his financial career, Jack attended Texas Technological University before going on to enlist in the U.S. Navy. He was discharged in 1960 with the rank of Lieutenant Commander.

Soon after his encounter with Preston and Al, Glen telephoned his father and told him that these two were claiming that he had been the administrative director of the mind control and time travel experiments known as the Montauk Project. They claimed that Jack had been in charge of financially supervising the projects as well as the hiring, firing, and paying of personnel. Jack's reply was "Well, stranger things have happened," and he promptly hung up on his son.

Glen's stepmother later told him that Jack cried for almost a week straight after that exchange. Crying was highly uncharacteristic for Jack. She said that he was "really broken up over it" and that he abruptly took her on a trip to the Bahamas. Jack refused to speak to Glen for several months. This was also very unusual. Glen says, "It wasn't as if we'd had a bad conversation or that he'd owned up to or admitted anything."

Eventually, Glen was back on speaking terms with his father and he broached the subject of Montauk again. Jack launched into a quasi-hypothetical and oblique story, saying: "Well, son, what if you were struggling with several jobs to pay your way through college when the Navy approached you with a lucrative position?" Jack went on to elliptically describe how it was that he had come to work for Naval Intelligence and how he became involved in immensely secret projects, something Glen had never known about his dad before.

Jack did not flatly deny Preston and Al's statements, but he did say that if they were as high up in the projects as they claimed, they sure as hell wouldn't be talking about it. Jack scoffed that they must be "solder jockeys," mere techies with relatively low security clearances and little understanding of the bigger picture. He guessed that if mind control technology of the kind they said existed; then it had probably been used on them as they appeared to be rather confused. Jack requested that Glen send him copies of the Montauk Project book series so that he could make notes in the margins about which of their claims were true and which were disinformational.

In an ensuing conversation, Jack lambasted all proponents of the Montauk Project as "deranged." This was in reply to something I told Glen to ask him about: Al Bielek's claim that Jack still owed him $500,000 in back pay. Jack incredulously retorted, "Show me a pay stub. Show me proof that the Montauk Project ever happened!"

Glen looked back at his childhood and recollected that throughout his father's employment at Mutual of New

York, he made regular trips from Dallas to New York City. During some periods, his visits were monthly. At other times, his visits were quarterly. Preston and Al had noted this pattern without any prompting from Glen. Checking up on this later, Glen discovered that during these trips, Jack would often stay at his sister Joyce's house — on the east end of Long Island.

Although Jack will no longer discuss the Montauk Project, he has recently been forthcoming with Glen about his involvement in other high security experiments incorporating the use of that most Montaukian of widgets, the Surface Barrier Transistor. Since Glen's childhood, his dad would often tell him about his experience as a Lieutenant in the late 1950's aboard a minesweeper in Tokyo Harbor. The original story was that his vessel had run aground on some rocks due to a navigator's error. However, in response to Glen's increasing awareness of his activities, Jack recently amended this account. He now said that his crew had in actuality been running extremely secret tests of the ELF-generating capacity of the Surface Barrier Transistor. Jack says that his mission for Naval Intelligence was to use this advanced technology to track underwater UFOs and to map out an immense cavern structure beneath the floor of Tokyo Bay. There was apparently a big UFO base down there.

Jack explained that during World War II, and in the years following, there had been thousands of sightings of UFOs plunging into and emerging out of those waters; therefore, the Navy dispatched his crew on a secret mission to survey the area. One day, they were tracking a UFO with their Surface Barrier Transistor technology when the amphibious flying object turned on them and rammed right through their vessel and actually severed it in half. Luckily, there were no casualties, and the crew members were able to straggle onto lifeboats. Jack recalled that the bisected ship took an eerily long time to founder. It was almost as if the two halves of the boat were, for a time, being held up from beneath. Jack and some of his men were then tasked with donning scuba gear and setting explosives on the sunken hulls to prevent the Japanese — and/or the UFOs — from capturing the Navy's secret technology.

Jack's quirky behavior around the issue of the Montauk Project and his subsequent disclosures were certainly very strange. I suggested to Glen that perhaps his father's stories of Tokyo Bay were programmed false memories. Glen disagreed because Jack had pointedly told him that management was never brainwashed because "it would have been impossible (for the secret projects) to function if management was not fully aware." Instead, they were heavily conditioned to never discuss high security information. Indeed, this was Jack's main argument against what Preston and Al professed about their level of involvement in the Montauk Project. He said that if they had been in any kind of administrative or managerial positions, they would never have spoken publicly about it.

Of course, this does not rule out the possibility that Jack was deliberately feeding his son a disinformational yarn about a Tokyo Bay incident in order to discredit Glen and all stories about Jack Pruitt to be released in the future; however, Jack did say that a record of this incident could be retrieved through the Freedom of Information Act. This would be well worth investigating.

It is almost humorous to see how many connections the Pruitts have to every conspiracy you can imagine. For example, in a phone conversation in May of 1999, Glen's stepmother was very excited and proud to tell Glen about how Jack had just been made a "34th degree Mason." She told him they had flown to Dallas and that none other than George Bush, the former President of the United States, had performed the ritual. She spoke of the grand reception afterwards to which all of the wives of the officiating Masons were invited and how she'd had a wonderful time chatting with Barbara Bush for much of the evening.

The history of Glen's mother is also quite interesting. Viola Ruth Bowen was raised in what Glen describes as an "extremely strict, abusive, white trash Florida Mormon household" where one of her childhood punishments was to be locked in a closet swarming with huge palmetto bugs. When she was fourteen years old, she was caught kissing a boy on the family porch. Her father forced a shotgun wedding within forty-eight hours. The unconsummated marriage was annulled after she escaped from the honeymoon hotel's bathroom window and jumped on a bus to New York City.

On the day of Viola's funeral, Jack informed Glen that she had been married an additional five times prior to marrying him. She had borne one child with each husband before marrying Jack and giving birth to Glen and his sister. That his mother had left behind five children with five different men was certainly news to Glen. Stranger still was that the life of Joyce, Jack's sister, had a similar pattern. She'd been married seven times and had given birth to nine daughters. Incidentally, three of these daughters grew up to be idiot-savants. They were mathematical geniuses who were institutionalized because they could not take care of themselves.

The profiles of Viola and Joyce echo the lives described by some self-professed survivors of multigenerational ritual abuse cults. The survivors often come from families with outwardly Mormon or Masonic backgrounds. They claim that they were essentially bred to be (as well as to breed) mind-controlled operatives for the CIA's Project Monarch, an MK-ULTRA subproject which we discussed earlier in this book.

Viola Bowen was for years the chief loan officer at a branch of the Republic National Bank in Dallas. This is where she met Jack Pruitt. It is also interesting to note that Viola was for many years a big player in fund-raising for the Republican Party in Texas. She would often have dinner alone with bigwigs like Al Haig and Henry Kissinger. These facts eerily resonate with the information in *Tranceformation of America*, a book authored by alleged Project Monarch survivor Cathy O'Brien. In her book, Cathy describes the lurid behind-the-scenes shenanigans of the political fund-raising parties she attended in which virtually all the politicians, delegates, and party girls were either Monarch-programmed robots or the CIA "handlers" who controlled them.

There are many strange anecdotes in Glen's history. For the first seven years of his life, his grandfather, Lee Pruitt, refused to see his grandchildren by Jack. Glen remembers the first summer he spent with his grandparents at their ranch in Western Texas near the New Mexican border. It was 1968.

He asked his grandfather, "How come you didn't want to know me before?"

Lee Pruitt sat Glen down and said, "Well, it's not that I didn't want to know you. It's that I feel like your father sold out the human race, and I really didn't want anything to do with him. It took your grandmother quite a few years to convince me that I shouldn't hold that over you kids. So, even though I'm angry at your father and feel like he did something very despicable, I'm not going to cut you and your sister off. Glen, you're just too young to talk about it, and don't worry about it, but I'm sure, some day, you'll know."

When Glen was 13, he finally approached his father about this. Their hobby together was to build cars. On one particular day, they were working on a 32' Crisscraft boat with a flying bridge. He asked Jack why his grandfather thought that he had sold out the human race. Jack replied that it was something that had happened in the military, and it was something he felt he had to do at the time.

He grew pensive and said, "It was a different time then. What we had done was for the good of the whole world, not just the United States."

Glen asked, "What's that supposed to mean?"

Jack then made a joke. He said, "Well, Glen, there's just some things that if I told ya, I just might have to kill ya!"

Jack used to say that to his son a lot. Glen let it drop, but some fifteen years later, while attending his first UFO conference in Denver, this story came back to haunt him. Two other attendees noted Glen's name and told him that there was a Jack Pruitt who had been one of the signatories on the 1955 GREATA treaty. This is the same treaty that Phil Schneider would later refer to in all of his lectures: the legendary treaty between the U.S. Navy and the Zeta Reticuli Grey aliens. According to the legend, the basic terms of this agreement were that the Greys offered samples of their technology for the military to study and back-engineer in exchange for the right to abduct, study, and collect genetic samples of selected humans. Glen was horrified that these people were telling him this. He got away from them as soon as possible.

Shortly afterward, Glen was visiting his grandmother on her deathbed. She was in the final stages of Alzheimer's disease. When she heard the sound of his voice, it triggered a first-person litany in which she described some very unusual events from the summer of '68. These occurred during that first visit Glen and his little sister had with their grandparents. As if she were reliving the events, Glen's grandmother told of her husband, Lee, waking up and going over to the children's bedroom to check in on them only to find that neither of them were there.

Lee angrily grabbed his shotgun, muttering, "They won't take my kids!" and marched outside.

There was a UFO parked in the backyard. Lee went inside the ship, shot the aliens dead, grabbed his grandkids, and carried them back to the house. He then telephoned the Roswell base and told them to come over and pick up the alien craft or he was "going to call UPI."

Glen has no recollection of this event, but he does have a few recollections of face-to-face waking contact with small "cute" blue-gilled aliens. He also recalls two fully-conscious encounters with the notorious Semjase, the beautiful female Pleiadian ufonaut who figures in the contactee stories of both Billy Meier and Fred Bell. Glen also has fragmentary memories of being in underground bases on multiple occasions as well as memories of riding on the levitating magnetic-drive train system reported by others.

After doing regression work with an abduction investigator, Glen has discovered as many as forty layers of false memories over certain events in his life. Given what he is currently discovering about his family background, he cannot say for sure if all of the alien memories are real.

What Glen is certain of is that Lee Pruitt, besides being the chief resident chemist, was one of the founders of Champion Oil, a company well-known for their auto products. Champion has since been purchased by Mobil Oil. Lee Pruitt bequeathed to his grandchildren all of his Mobil stock and the patents to his designs of the drill bits, pumps, and oil refining processes still widely used in the petroleum industry. Today, these assets are worth potentially billions of dollars. Although Lee passed away over ten years ago, Jack, as the executor of Lee's will, has never distributed these assets to the heirs. The grandchildren are finally initiating a legal motion to discover what happened to these properties.

I will relate one last strange anecdote relating to another branch of the family because it underscores the Pruitts' connection to the Montauk legend. In 1997, while driving from Atlanta to New York, Glen stayed over with his cousins in South Carolina. The home had originally been that of Jack's brother, Martin Pruitt, before he died. That afternoon, while he was rummaging through some boxes in the basement, Glen accidentally backed into a wood-paneled wall which turned out to be set on a pivot. A plaster seal at the corner crumbled and the wall swung open. A loudly buzzing fluorescent light cracked to life in a secret room where there was a thick layer of dust over everything. The room appeared to have been sealed since Martin's death in 1977. Inside, Glen was shocked to see what looked like a Montauk Chair. It was a metal chair with electrodes for the head, spine and wrists. The legs of the chair were embedded within four large Tesla coils. The room also contained a huge tape-drive D.E.C. Mini-Vax computer. Strangely, the model of the computer appeared to be from the mid 1980's, well after Uncle Martin's death. On the wall were physics notes, power curve graphs, a poster of the cabalistic Tree of Life, and yellowed photographs taken in the 1930's.

Glen discerned the era of the computer from having worked in the computer hardware industry for several years, including a stint at Texas Instruments. Being a car enthusiast, he determined the dating of the pictures by closely inspecting the cars in the background. The clothes and hairstyles were also clearly of the 1930's. One of the photos was a group picture of Tesla, Lee Pruitt, and his

Uncle Martin as an adult. This was highly peculiar since Martin would have been only two years old in 1935, the approximate year in which the shot was taken.

Glen did not mention this shocking find to his cousins because he felt embarrassed to have been snooping around their house; however, continuing on his journey northwards, Glen could not contain himself from speaking about these oddities to a friend over a pay phone from the road.

He carried on mulling over the implications of these objects in his uncle's house as he drove to New York. It had only been a few weeks since he'd had the strange encounter with Preston and Al and heard the story of his father's involvement in Montauk for the first time. A few days after he arrived in New York, he finally got up the nerve to call his cousins and to ask them about that secret room with the chair and the strange equipment. They replied that a new septic system had just been installed for the house and that the room and the small hill adjacent to the house were now gone.

Well before the publication of this book, Glen forwarded a rough draft of this chapter to Jack Pruitt for his inspection and approval. Jack's response was that it was very interesting, and he had no corrections. He then offered to give Glen the details of the U.S. Navy's agreement with the Greys except that it was to be written in a fictional format.

Several months later, in March of 2000, I had the pleasure of joining Glen for lunch with Jack and his wife during their visit to New York City. Glen had warned me not to discuss the Montauk Project or the Greys as Jack would not tolerate this sort of talk in front of his fundamentalist wife. So, I politely asked Jack about the period of his life when he had lived in New York.

Jack responded that he attended NYU Business School classes in 1961 at the building on 1 Wall Street. This was on top of working full-time for Republic National Bank and starting a family. He told me that he was so busy during that time of his life that he barely remembers it. Actually, it was his wife who pointed that out to me before Jack echoed the statement. (I found her interpolation of this comment a bit odd since the two did not even meet until some 30 years later.)

Jack said that he had looked for the building on Wall Street on a previous visit to New York but was surprised to note that the building was no longer there. He went on to tell me that he had lived in Jackson Heights, Queens. This is where Glen was born. He warmly described Glen as a bouncing baby and pointed out how his blonde first wife had stuck out in the neighborhood which at that time was made up almost entirely of Orthodox Jews.

It was a pleasant lunch characterized by small talk and peppered with clues. Jack had read the chapter I wrote about him and was nice as could be to me. I believe that a door for future more in-depth conversations has been opened.

The aggregate impact of these circumstances over his lifetime, catalyzed by his encounter with Preston and Al, have opened the floodgates of Glen's understanding about his family, himself, and indeed, the entire multiverse.

9

REALITY

If Phil Schneider and his family were involved in an ostensible interaction between elements of the U.S. military and off-planetary intelligence, then Glen Pruitt and his family, who are still living, appear to be even more deeply enmeshed. Both families are examples of secret sectors weaving their way mysteriously into the fabric of multigenerational consciousness.

The Phil Schneider story compels us to ask what is real. As unreal as his stories sounded to the average American, something Phil said evidently got him killed. This has resulted in the "martyr syndrome" whereby the fact of his murder and its obvious cover-up bolster the possibility that at least some of what he was saying was dangerously true.

Phil Schneider's lectures were essentially about an alien invasion of our world and the alien manipulation of our government. The testimonies of dozens of other people support much of what Phil was saying. Other underground base experiencers and proponents of this belief, such as Al Bielek, Stewart Swerdlow, and Glen Pruitt, all have their insights into Phil Schneider's testimonies and the larger story of which they were a part.

The alien invasion story could be described as the emerging myth of our time. It is a legend that pervades our current popular culture. It has been propagated in numerous TV shows and films such as the *X-Files, Dark Skies,* and *Independence Day* as well as the underground cult hit series by Sky Books about the Montauk Project. This modern-day myth is particularly compelling because its proponents sometimes end up threatened or murdered.

Whether or not one believes in an actual alien invasion, it is without question that aliens have invaded our popular culture. A look at this phenomenon beautifully illustrates how the experiences of the individual impact and contribute to the construction of mass consciousness or consensus "reality."

Since the late 1940's, an increasing number of people began to report strange sightings and experiences with alien beings and their technology. Over the years, the population processed this information in accordance with their own personal experiences and mindsets. When the information was in violation of everything an individual held to be "true," that individual tended to judge the report to be "insane," "a lie," "fictional," or "drug-related." If the person had never had that particular experience but could at least conceive of it happening, that person's response was to deem the story "possible" or to even go as far as to "believe" it. Those who had actually had similar experiences "knew" that there was "truth" to the story. Thus, the information entered the public debate in mass consciousness and within fifty years, The *X-Files* had become a successful TV show spawning scores of other shows like it. Consequently, more people today believe in an alien presence on Earth than was the case fifty years ago.

Glen Pruitt is one person who did not need a TV show to inform him of the possibility of off-planetary beings visiting earth. Glen Pruitt's own life story and his unique insights offer a fascinating perspective on both Phil Schneider's life and on the legendary relationship between the military and the aliens.

10

QUANTUM REALITIES

In befriending Glen Pruitt and investigating Phil Schneider's life, I noted that they shared some things in common. Each had fathers who were Naval officers and were involved in matters of high security. Besides that, Glen and Phil both reported having unusual encounters with alien beings and having experiences in underground military bases. It is also noteworthy that they both had uncommon extrasensory abilities.

Phil Schneider's ex-wife, Cynthia, reports that when she and Phil would dig for rare stones while engaging in their shared hobby of mineralogy, he would tell her that he could actually "hear" the agates. Phil's method for finding agates would be to listen for them. He would start digging where the sound was coming from and promptly unearth the gemstones.

Glen Pruitt's paranormal abilities are also very developed. As he has earned a living for many years as a psychic healer, I thought it might be interesting to get a "reading" from him about Phil Schneider. At the least, he might offer some insights into the situation. My intent was to gain a perspective on Phil's and others' claims about underground base activities to see if I could make some sense out of them. I had no idea the can of worms that Glen's reading would open up. The first thing Glen had to say about Phil sounded even more insane to me than Phil's own stories. He said that most of the unusual experiences Phil described in his lectures had taken place in a parallel universe. I thought there was no way that I could communicate what Glen was saying to a discerning public while maintaining his credibility, not to mention my own. His readings seemed way too far out.

Then it dawned on me that there had been a hit show on television for several years, which I had never watched, called *Sliders* that dealt almost exclusively with the topic of parallel universes. Around the same time, a book was released written by David Deutsch, an extremely well respected mathematician who is a member of the Quantum Computation and Cryptography Research Group at Oxford University and a winner of the Paul Dirac Medal and Prize. The book is called *The Fabric of Reality: The Science of Parallel Universes and Its Implications*. In it, Deutsch theorizes on the existence and workings of parallel universes from the standpoint of theoretical physics and virtual reality computer programs. It soon became apparent to me that the discussion of parallel universes is a staple of Quantum Physics and that alternate universes had long ago been predicted by Albert Einstein in his Black Hole Theory.

From the perspective of Western consensus reality, it is acceptable for a physicist to theorize about parallel universes. From the standpoint of the pseudo-ideology of political correctness, it is deemed either quaint or "empowering" for shamans from Native cultures to discuss their knowledge of what could scientifically be termed parallel universes. However, when a Western person with no institutional credentials, no fancy math or ethnicity to hide behind describes his or her direct experiences of parallel universes, he or she is branded as a schizophrenic — period.

Needless to say, this is how I was beginning to regard my friend Glen. The question also arose as to how others were beginning to regard *me* when I would simply discuss his readings. Anyway, I allowed him to forge ahead deriving some comfort in the knowledge that both the "lowest common denominator" that is television and the highest of the high brow institutions, Oxford, were both espousing the concept of parallel universes.

Glen's worldview incorporates quantum concepts and sheds a new light on the information that is currently circulating about Phil Schneider, the Montauk Project, underground bases, alien abduction, Satanic ritual abuse, and New World Order conspiracy theories. It is Glen's opinion that neither the Dulce Wars nor the Montauk Project occurred or are occurring in our timeline or universe. As he sees it, the Dulce Wars are taking place in a parallel world adjacent to our own and the Montauk Projects are an ongoing series of time travel, mind control, and genocidal experiments that are occurring not here but in many universes parallel to our own. However, there are important cognitive effects or echoes of these events that *are* being felt here.

Glen says that most people with claims of experiences of this nature are having "bleedthrough" memories from their alternate selves. He explains that these perceived events are real; they're just not happening in this particular space/time continuum. The brutal realities that have been termed "recovered memories" by some experiencers are actually the memories of their alternate selves in a Nazi culture that has a strong foothold in roughly 90 universes close in vibration to ours. A small amount of these people, he says, may actually be what he calls "crossovers," people who were brought here via time travel technology from one of these "Montaukian" universes for one reason or another.

These parallel universe events are affecting the consciousness of people in our reality. The bleedthrough experience can be very strong for some people; such that it actually feels to them as if these events actually happened to them in this reality. Those who have been subject to government brainwashing would have an especially difficult time distinguishing between realities. This is what may have been the case with Phil Schneider, Preston Nichols, Al Bielek and others. Glen is adamant that most of these people's bizarre memories did not occur to their bodies in this timeline and that it is crucial to the healing process of those who are troubled by these experiences to understand this: these memories are not truly their own.

When I told Preston Nichols of Glen's views on this, he said that Glen was a disinformant who was involved in covering up the human rights abuses that have been occurring right here in our very own universe. Given Glen's family background, that would not be hard to imagine. As previously mentioned, Glen has recently discovered that there are patches of his own memory and awareness that appear to have been distorted by elements of the intelligence community. However, he does not intentionally seek to disinform the public.

Glen's understanding of the workings of parallel universes is somewhat different from what is propounded in contemporary theoretical physics by David Deutsch and others. The current scientific thinking, known as the Many Worlds Interpretation, is that the universe is constantly splitting off into infinite copies of itself generated by the actions or movements of every being and everything in it. In other words, countless universes are perpetually being observer-created. Every micromoment is a parallel universe unto itself.

In quantum mechanics, an electron is considered not only to POTENTIALLY be anywhere at any time within the electron shell in orbit around an atom's nucleus, it IS anywhere at any time; not just within the orbital path of the shell but outside of the shell's confines as well. This blows apart any classical common sense ideas of space and time.

The Many Worlds Interpretation is Quantum Mechanics on a larger scale where it is theorized that every possibility in reality IS happening. Copies of universes are perpetually being generated, each one being just as real as the one we each perceive to be the real universe. "We" (down to the smallest subatomic particle) are each perceiving and creating infinite parallel universes constantly.

Not everyone in the physics community accepts the MWI, but it is currently the cutting edge scientific explanation for how reality works. There are also mathematical theorems and particle accelerator experiments that have seemingly proven it. The Many Worlds Interpretation does not make a distinction between all the potential universes which it says are constantly "branching off" and the "one" universe most human beings commonly perceive themselves to inhabit. To the MWI, all these copy universes are equally real. We only perceive ourselves to be in one of them at any particular time.

This is not so in Glen's cosmology which distinguishes between different kinds of parallel universes. He agrees with the Many Worlds Interpretation's concept of the endless creation of possible universes or "ante-universes," but he also sees the existence of "prime" parallel universes. Prime universes are much more stable, coherent, and substantial than the infinitely branching-off copy universes which he sees as spiralling off of the mass consciousness trajectories of the primes and dissipating into nonexistence just as rapidly as they are created. Both Glen and the MWI agree that we each have myriad versions of ourselves simultaneously existing on these parallel worlds. These "alternate selves" are locked into similar time-track illusions but with slightly different variables in each reality (that is, if our other versions haven't died yet).

The prime parallel universes described by Glen have the familiar firmament-type structure that we have been acculturated to perceive as "reality" in the West. According to Glen, these prime parallel firmaments have been in existence since the beginning of our multiverse. In addition to prime universes and possible universes, he also acknowledges the existence of digitally-mastered artificial parallel universes that others have also reported to have been generated by groups such as the Montauk Project. All of these types of universes are real, but they possess different qualities and magnitudes of reality having to do with the character and amount of consciousness/energy associated with them.

These distinctions are inconsistent with the Many Worlds Interpretation which describes all of the infinite parallel universes as being equally valid or having the same degree of reality. It will be interesting to see if future mathematical work and experiments directly probing the interplay between consciousness/energy and physical reality eventually arrive at similar distinctions between types of universes.

11

QUANTUM MONTAUKS

The following paragraphs summarize Glen Pruitt's views on the multidimensional dramas of the Montauk Project. I am including this information because it serves as a background for his reading of what happened to Phil Schneider. It is also possible that some of Glen's beliefs or that the entirety of his ornate Montaukian cosmology could be the product of a complex denial mechanism. Given what is alleged about his father's activities, Glen's outlook could even be an expression of government programming. Regardless of their ultimate origin, his observations are informative of a kind of quantum consciousness. His insights are especially interesting because they have found some corroboration in the reports of Montauk Project survivors and other multidimensional visionaries who I have spoken with. Were all of these people mind controlled by the same MK-ULTRA team? What is the "real" truth to these readings? These are some things to keep in mind in regards to this highly provocative information.

It is Glen's understanding that the Montauk Projects that most affect us are those being generated from a parallel universe that he refers to as Montauk Prime. Some Montauk Project survivors have reported experiencing this reality, a world where the Nazis won World War II and which is to this day dominated by a totalitarian and fascistic military government hell-bent on controlling all the other parallel worlds that it can.

The Montauk Project that is described in the Sky Books series took place in a universe very similar and close in vibration to our own, a universe he calls Montauk 5. This world contains a colonial outpost of Montauk Prime. It is a reality where the Nazis have a stronger presence than on our own world although they are still secret and underground. The Nazis of Montauk 5 are located primarily in a base beneath the Antarctica of that world. They are trying to manipulate events from behind the scenes in order to eventually take over that world. They sometimes do bizarre time travel experiments (with aid from the Nazis of Montauk Prime) in their attempts to do so. Montauk 5 is the reality that Glen believes Preston, Al, and others have gotten confused with our own.

This neighbor world of Montauk 5 could be seen as a staging area for the planned invasion of our own universe by this multidimensional Nazi culture. The version of Jack Pruitt in Montauk 5 was the director of the Montauk Project that Preston and Al recognize. The Jack Pruitt on our world was *not* the director of the Project here because it never happened here. Glen's belief is that Preston and Al are having bleedthrough memories from versions of themselves that were involved in the Montauk Project in the Montauk 5 universe and that is how they recognize Jack's photo.

Glen suggests that the driving force behind Nazi-type activities on our world does not entirely originate in our universe. Trevor Ravenscroft, author of *The Spear Of Destiny*, a popular book about the occult aspects of the Nazi party, makes a similar proposition: that the impetus for the hell on Earth that was unleashed by the Nazis in WW II had its origins in another dimension.

Glen's view is that Nazis from parallel universes have come here and set up secret bases on our world. The locations of the more important of these bases have been beneath Antarctica and, briefly, within the mountains of Bavaria during the 1930's. He says that there continues to be a small presence in one of the buildings at Area 51, and there is also the base beneath Tokyo Bay which was referred to in the previous chapter. It is now mostly abandoned.

There is an interdimensional space station in orbit around Earth, not fully in phase with this universe, which is run by Nazis from Montauk Prime. Glen says that this space station is beaming mind control frequencies to satellites contracted by the LTV Company (which is fully in our world). He suggests that the L.A. riots were induced by microwave mind control signals emanating from these satellites, an example of an interdimensional Montaukian manipulation of our reality. This reading does have an eerie resonance to it given the racial polarizing that this event both reflected and engendered.

He goes on to say that many sighted UFOs have often been the craft of multidimensional humans rather than those of "aliens." Interestingly, this view corresponds with the testimony of Barney Hill of the landmark 1961 abduction case. On the tape recording of the hypnotic regression of his abduction episode, Hill originally described the captain of the flying saucer he was taken aboard as "a German Nazi." In later accounts, the captain was described as a Grey alien.

The physical Montaukian presence on our world has been considerably reduced in recent years consisting, for the most part, of unmanned "interdimensional weather monitoring stations" which measure the magnetic space/time/gravitic fluctuations of the key portal areas on Earth. The particularities of the time travel technology used by this regressive Montaukian group require that they constantly gauge these subtle changes at certain wormhole sites in every parallel universe they have access to. Such sites on our Earth include locations at Montauk, South Africa, Turkey, China, and others.

Perhaps Glen's most radical claim is that the most secret of the Black Budget projects today involve the underground archeological reclamation of ancient Atlantean technology. He says that the media's willingness to address the UFO and abduction phenomena is merely a smokescreen to hide this much bigger secret: that most of the other-dimensional and alien activity occurring in our reality directly relates to these entities' agendas to recover buried Atlantean technologies on our world.

Another parallel universe that has a great influence on ours is a world Glen calls America Prime. On this world, the American involvement in World War II never happened. The Japanese never bombed Pearl Harbor. The Germans never invaded England as a truce was arrived at between the British and the Germans. American culture there is very gung-ho and similar to what it was like on our world during the 1940's with a sense of justified self-righteousness. That world, however, has had plenty of other problems. The entire city of Chicago was flattened in a nuclear accident in the 1930's. In the late 1960's, Los Angeles was completely destroyed in a drawn-out underground war with aliens that continues there to this day.

America Prime is the world that Glen believes Phil Schneider and others have spoken about when recounting their experiences in the Dulce Wars or any underground war with aliens. He does not see an underground war occurring on our world at all. In the parallel world of

America Prime, the Montauk Project is no secret to American citizens. The public acknowledges it as a form of defense against the interdimensional incursions from both the Greys and the Montauk Prime Nazis, both representing ongoing battles on that world. Glen says that secret factions in our military on this world have recently made an alliance with entities from the America Prime universe in a bid to get their help in unearthing our Atlantean technology which we would, in turn, share with them.

Glen's reading of Phil Schneider is that he was an individual who was suffering from the effects of several extraordinary circumstances which had left Phil very confused. Phil was involved in Black Projects on our world as a geologist, and he was exposed to strange scenarios involving the U.S. Government's collaboration with aliens. Phil was also involved in extremely high security archeological projects aimed at reclaiming ancient Atlantean technology buried deep beneath the ground. Phil was brainwashed upon being discharged from these projects thus compounding the ongoing psychological trauma from all of his exposure to aliens.

Glen also sees that the Phil Schneider of the America Prime universe was killed in a nuclear explosion during a skirmish with Grey aliens. Something very anomalous resulted from his death by nuclear explosion on that world: the personality of that version of Phil ended up melding with his personality in this world. Phil had two versions of his personality within the same body which is something that his wife did notice.

Like the Phil Schneider on this world, the America Prime version of Phil had also been involved in underground base projects but in a world where the political alliances between the military and the various alien groups were vastly different from what they are here. For example, on our world (Glen says), a sector of the military has a secret alliance with Grey alien groups; whereas, in America Prime, we are openly at war with them. This is what fueled Phil's outrage at seeing our government here collaborate with Grey aliens. Phil's America Prime personality, which had grafted itself onto his original one here, perceived the Greys as the vilest enemy and he could not comprehend any sort of diplomatic arrangement with them.

Glen's reading of the Montauk saga does have some radical departures from the legends propounded by its avowed survivors. I sent his readings to one such survivor, Stewart Swerdlow, author of *Montauk: The Alien Connection, The Healer's Handbook*, and a gifted mentalist himself. He surprised me by saying that he agreed with much of what Glen had to say except for some salient points which he wanted to discuss with me in person.

Over a delicious lunch prepared by his wife, Janet, Stewart told me about a recent trip he took lecturing in Florida. A friend of his had told him that he absolutely must look up an acquaintance of his while he was there, a man I'll call Mr. Smith. Stewart called up Mr. Smith, and they arranged to meet in a diner.

Stewart's jaw dropped when in walked a man who looked exactly like his father. Mr. Smith was equally struck by Stewart's remarkable resemblance to his own son. Stewart learned that Mr. Smith lived a rather mysterious life traveling across the country in a recreational vehicle with his pretty wife who appeared to be at least thirty years his junior.

That was only the beginning. Mr. Smith spoke with Stewart and showed him photos of an underground temple in New Mexico, the walls of which were adorned with the exact same hyperspacial symbols that Stewart discusses in his workshops.

Stewart gives classes on what he calls the "hyperspatial language," a system of runelike pictograms which he believes to be the unconscious telepathic language of all sentient beings. Just prior to his meeting with Mr. Smith, a strange man had arrived late to one of his lectures and then promptly fell asleep. During the break, the man awoke and showed Stewart the same photos that Mr. Smith was showing him. After showing Stewart the photos, the strange man apologized and said that he had to leave the lecture. This was after having paid for the full workshop and sleeping through the first half.

Back in the Florida diner, Mr. Smith proceeded to tell Stewart that the temple in the photo had been constructed around 800 A.D. in our timeline by beings from the 28th Century of a parallel universe. Stewart thought to himself, "Great! My friend has set me up to have lunch with a madman!" Mr. Smith then proceeded to say that he himself had been sent to our world from the 28th Century of the above-mentioned parallel universe to stop a nuclear accident from wiping out Chicago in our 1930's, an event which had occurred in his timeline. His mission here was a success, and he has been here ever since.

When Stewart read Glen's description of a nuclear accident wiping out Chicago in a parallel universe, his hair stood on end. Nonetheless, he did disagree with some things Glen said. Stewart steadfastly maintains that the Montauk Project, as it is described in the books (of which his is one), *did* occur in this timeline. He agrees, however, that there is interaction between parallel versions of the project and that the Nazis are a multidimensional Luciferian expression of consciousness with off-world origins.

I have also noted a vast body of very strange corroborated information regarding the Montauk Project, alien abductions, and underground bases, most of which I have not included in this book. These stories cannot merely be chalked up to the schizophrenia of various individuals. As bizarre as these reports seem, people (who do not know each other and who are otherwise sane and fully functioning) confirm them with their own experiences of the same scenarios. Moreover, the combined pattern of the numerous reports keeps pointing to a bigger story involving an Atantlean civilization in Earth's prehistory and a "New World Order" agenda for our future with off-planetary influence all around. This New World Order agenda was one of the main themes of Phil Schneider's lectures before he was killed.

12

THE NEW WORLD ORDER

*"The world can therefore seize the oppor-
tunity [Persian Gulf crisis] to fulfill the
long-held promise of a New World Order
where diverse nations are drawn together
in common cause to achieve the universal
aspirations of mankind."*
— George Herbert Walker Bush

What, exactly is the New World Order? George
Bush invokes the concept of a New World Order in order to
paint a picture of a positive nearby future with uncharted
vistas of multilateral world government cooperation.
Perpetual Presidential candidate Pat Buchanan bandies
this term about with a less than warm and friendly conno-
tation. He has propounded for years, in prime time
soundbites, about an impending "New World Order" which
he says threatens to wipe out all that is good in America.
Can these two men, who shared the same podium at a
Republican National Convention, possibly be speaking
about the same thing?

The New World Order obviously means different
things to different people; therefore, it is not truly fair to

call it the New World Order. In the most general sense, the New World Order signifies a future alignment of world power which is not clearly distinguished at this time. Some people dread it while others welcome it—whatever it is.

In conspiracy literature, the grandaddy of all other conspiracies is that of the New World Order. For years, fringe publications and the Internet have hosted an epidemic of strident and often disjointed references to an imminent worldwide "secret government" clampdown. The inherent vagueness of the subject and the heated shrillness it inspires in its proponents has caused some wags to refer to it the New World Odor! History, however, has shown that there are power-mad individuals who have managed to galvanize nations into coming close to actualizing their own versions of the New World Order. Hitler and his posse would be the prime example.

Phil Schneider's chief claim was that of having been a seventeen year employee of corporations that were at the core of the New World Order conspiracy. He railed against the New World Order but never fully explained who or what it was although he could hardly be blamed for his perplexity. The bewildering plot of the so-called New World Order conspiracy is so convoluted and outrageous that it may never be clearly explained or understood. One must also consider that if Phil's claims of being an erstwhile functionary of the New World Order were true, then one of the hazards of such employment, unbeknownst to him, may have included a brainwashing that made his telling of the tale all that much more difficult.

In conspiracy literature, the New World Order is generally referred to as a master plan for a fascist world government. With great indignation, supporters of this conspiracy theory claim that the groundwork for this plan is currently being laid, largely at the taxpayers' expense, without their consent or awareness. NATO bombings and UN troop movements are invoked as outward evidence for the escalation of the New World Order agenda as are stories of secret concentration camps being built on American soil, railroad cars loaded with shackles, and mysterious military receipts for the importation of thousands of guillotines. New World Order watchdogs warn that if we do not take steps to investigate and to stop these activities, we will one day wake up subject to martial law and worse: we will get herded into concentration camps.

The typical NWO tract warns about a looming disastrous upheaval. They say that this cataclysmic scenario will actually be an event which has been carefully staged years in advance by the "grand conspirators" whose operatives have infiltrated branches of every world government. This tumultuous occurrence could be anything from a stock market crash to a terrorist nuclear attack. The end result will be the declaration of a National Emergency by the Federal Government which will precipitate the implementation of various Presidential Executive Orders.

These Executive Orders, which have been signed by the likes of Nixon, Bush, and Clinton over the years, completely suspend all Constitutional rights. The Federal Emergency Management Agency, better known as FEMA, is empowered by the Executive Orders to confiscate all private property and seize control of all of the fuel, transportation, and food in the country. FEMA may separate families and forcibly confine citizens in any one of 43 internment camps which have already been built for this purpose. The Executive Orders which specifically enact all of the above are all apparently in the Federal Register in Washington D.C., numbered 10995 through 12919, and anyone can request a copy of them.

Almost everyone in America has had the experience, at least once, of watching television and witnessing an announcement which declares something to the effect of, "This is a test of the Emergency Broadcast System. This is only a test. If this had been an actual emergency, we would have alerted you to report to your local authorities..." whereupon a tone is sounded. The Emergency Broadcast System may very well be related to Executive Order 10995 which "Provides for the seizure of all communications media in the United States."

It would be the United States government's ultimate undertaking, in the interest of preserving its preeminent standing in the world, to have well-laid plans for a worst case scenario such as a nuclear holocaust, asteroid hit, or some other form of economic collapse. Conspiracy whistleblowers warn, however, that our government has been infiltrated by nefarious elements that would invoke these Executive Orders at the moment that they finally unmask their party's intentions to overtly take over the United States and the world. They remind us that Executive Orders 9066 and 9102 in 1942 provided for the removal of over 110,000 Japanese-Americans from their homes in Pacific Coast states for their relocation into ten internment camps specifically built for them throughout America's Southwest.

Conspiracy theorists, such as popular radio show host David Emory, say that this clandestine invasion of our military/intelligence agencies has its origin in a secret alliance made toward the end of WW II between the Nazi General Reinhard Gehlen and OSS Chief Allen Dulles. This pact led directly to the creation of the CIA in 1947. The core of this new intelligence agency was made up of former Nazi SS officers who were issued new identities by the U.S. Government.

There is a certain ring of truth to this scenario when one considers the CIA's involvement over the years in destabilizing third world governments and replacing them with fascist puppet dictatorships. Could it really be that the CIA has operated as a front for the Nazi SS working toward the Nazi agenda of world domination in a covert manner under the aegis of its former enemy, the United States government? Could it really be that so very few of its employees, not to mention the country's leadership and citizens, are aware of this actuality?

Black Ops, Black Budget Projects, and underground bases are said by conspiratologists to be the primary domain of this clandestine and modern-day Fourth Reich. Where tax money is insufficient to fund this secret underground base empire and the testing of its super technologies, the illegal drug trade pays for the rest in a triangle of drugs-for-money-for-weapons that has driven wars in Vietnam, Afghanistan, the former Yugoslavia, and numerous conflicts in Latin America. There is much well-documented evidence about the CIA's ongoing involvement in the trade of cocaine and heroin and more information keeps leaking out.

Congress apparently has absolutely no power over this secret government world of Black Budget projects and drug money laundering because the Congressmen assigned to "oversee" them do not have the security clearances to know what's really going on. Black Ops and any other government activities sanctioned by the National Security Act, by definition, operate outside of the U.S. Constitution and The Bill of Rights. No wonder some people are paranoid!

Many proponents of the New World Order claim to be either former high security personnel or claim to have contact with such people. It would stand to reason that some of these other ex-intelligence employees, like Phil, may have gone through their own "debriefing" sessions. Taking their first or second hand testimonies with a grain of salt might be advisable. However, the aggregate sum of these declarations do form a general pattern which, combined with various clues leaked in the media over the years, do make me pause to consider whether there really is a "secret government" in operation that is funded with the multibillion-dollar worldwide drug trade. These leaks include the Iran Contra Scandal of the 1980's which linked the Reagan White House with the unsanctioned and illegal peddling of arms and cocaine to support right wing insurgents in Central America.

The 1996 investigative reporting by Pulitzer Prize-winner Gary Webb in the *San Jose Mercury News* powerfully substantiated that the CIA was heavily involved in the Los Angeles crack trade of the 1980's. Webb's series of articles led to an uproar in the Afro-American community culminating in a bizarre and unprecedented nationally-televised "Town Hall" type of meeting held in the predominantly Black Los Angeles neighborhood of Compton. The current Director of the CIA at the time, John Deutsch, attempted to reassure the area's residents on live television that the CIA would never have condoned the sale of drugs to local gangs. Deutsch was soon sacked from his job and has since lost his security clearance as well. It really makes you wonder.

13

THE PHYSICS OF INSANITY

The main argument used to dismiss the claims of Phil Schneider, Al Bielek or any percipient of the extraordinary is that these claimants are insane; therefore, nothing they say is valid. I believe this is a lazy knee-jerk way to avoid dealing with the unsettling implications of their information.

That the hegemony would label such folks as "insane" is a bit of the pot calling the kettle black, especially since the scientific belief system of Western civilization could itself be viewed as a form of sanctioned insanity. The most fundamental "objective" scientific assumptions about existence, of which Darwinism and the Many Worlds Interpretation of Quantum Mechanics are prime examples, is that reality is a myriad of systems that replicate themselves echoing ad infinitum — all by accident and for no particular reason.

This current predominating scientific worldview, which grew out of the very Age of Reason itself, purports that there is no "reason" for any of the stuff we call reality! The ideology is insane, by definition. To be fair, this is no crazier than any other allegory or dogma which has gamely assayed to ascertain the enigma of existence. Try as we might to explain "it all," the human quandary is that we do not really know who we are, what is going on, or why. The elaborateness of any theory or fable can but momentarily soothe bumbling humans from their collective predicament of utter confusion — and yes, the precipice of insanity!

The Many Worlds Interpretation of Quantum Mechanics, although schismatic from the creaky old orthodox scientific doctrine of causality, does represent the fullest flowering of scientific thought. This math-based explication of reality actually confirms the claims of certain over-the-edge paranoia-mongers. For example, there are pesky assertions that the Queen Mother is a shapeshifting reptilian — and a cannibalistic practitioner of satanism, too!

Modern math validates the most far-out allegations of even the most whacked conspiracy evangelist. It also supports every outlandish thing ever asserted by Phil Schneider, David Icke, and every alien abductee and Montauk Project survivor. Why? Because on a quantum level, every possibility is TRUE.

While I agree with the fundamental quantum principle that everything is possible and therefore "real" on some level, it appears that a certain Orwellian condition obtains whereby some realities are more "true" than others. It is patently observable that the "truth" or pervasiveness of any given belief corresponds to the amount of consciousness energy associated with it. As far as I am aware, this has yet to be factored into the MWI theory.

In the discussion of the MWI, the relevance of mass consciousness energy cannot be overlooked; yet, to the best of my knowledge, it officially has been. This factor is what makes advertising, public relations, "positioning," "perception," marketing, and other forms of mind control so important to people with huge profits to be made by paying for these services. The more consciousness energy entrained into a concept, the more "real" or "true" that it appears and occurs. Thought and belief generate reality. It is that simple.

We have asked the question, "What is reality?" and discussed the MWI that hazards to answer this most profound of questions. Simply put, the MWI says that the multiverse is a system of various fields of consciousness interacting with one another and constantly generating infinite fields of consciousness or "observer-created realities" in relation to one another.

So, if all is consciousness, and if all is relative, the next questions would seem to be: "What, exactly is insanity?" This question has been central to the life work of Olga Kharitidi, M.D., a Russian psychiatrist who was born into a family of several generations of medical doctors. She is the author of a marvelous book, *Entering the Circle*, in which she describes her experiences as a doctor in a Siberian psychiatric hospital.

Dr. Kharitidi was treating incurably insane patients with the orthodox methodology of drugs and getting the predictably dismal results until she had an unexpected encounter with a shaman in the Altai mountain region. This encounter triggered a series of events whereby her consciousness was opened up to alternate healing practices that supplemented her psychiatric training. Happily, this led to a much higher rate of success with her schizophrenic patients.

Synchronistically, she became acquainted with the director of a Siberian physics laboratory, Dr. Ivan Petrovich Dmitriev, a man who had been applying his research in quantum physics to the study of reality. Dmitriev and his team had constructed a mirrored cylindrical psychotronic chamber devised to "open up states of alternate awareness." Dr. Kharitidi agreed to participate in a consciousness experiment that he and his team were running with this equipment.

During individual forays within the chamber, both she and Dmitriev each experienced similar visions about alternate streams of human development. Dmitriev perceived that some of these alternate reality streams were currently physically intersecting with our own reality. The manifestations of this occurrence were in the form of recent archaeological discoveries of mummies in the Altai region, information of which had been reported in the news. Dmitriev received a powerful impression that these mummies were NOT from our timeline and that they had somehow emerged into our world from a parallel earth.

Kharitidi's account is interesting, all the more so because it is a vastly unrelated source for a report of parallel universes; not to mention the apparent collision of a parallel world into our own. On the Internet, most references to parallel timelines "colliding" with ours can be found on conspiracy-related sites bearing stories that relate to the Philadelphia Experiment and the Montauk Project. These accounts are often contained in "channeled" messages ascribed to extraterrestrial beings or in tracts by people who profess insider knowledge of such events. Other current legends about parallel universes and interdimensional travel can be found under the keywords "Ong's Hat" and "Damanhur."

The legend of the Ong's Hat travel cult was originally posted on the Internet in 1991 by Joseph Matheny as the "Incunabula Papers" during the earliest days of BBS and Internet communications. In a series of documents, the reader discovers how a ragtag team of maverick misfits (Black Muslims, bikers, runaway kids, Sufis, drug dealers, lesbians, computer hackers, quantum physicists, and chaos math whizzes) formed a commune in the New Jersey Pine Barrens and built the "Egg." This glistening Faberge-like device is said to have enabled transdimensional travel into completely unpopulated and pristine mirror worlds. Imagine a New Jersey devoid of suburban sprawl, pollution, or any trace of human activity at all! Apparently, it is a beautiful place. But, there is a dark side to the Ong's Hat story.

Around the time of the early 1980's, the New Jersey Pine Barrens commune was reportedly stormed by a Delta Force team from nearby Fort Dix. These shock troops are said to have toted flame-throwers and automatic weaponry as they descended from ropes off of helicopters. In a precursor to the Branch Davidian massacre, the Ong's Hat commune was burned down to the ground and as many as seven cult members were killed. It never made the papers.

On a completely different note, Damanhur is today a thriving artistic alchemical mystery school located in the Northwest of Italy whose members claim to have mastered time travel. Open to visitors, it is located atop what is purportedly one of the most powerful vortexes on the planet. The community members have carved out of a mountainside, which consists largely of the rare earth element millenite, a completely breathtaking "Temple of Mankind" that has been called the Tenth Wonder of the World. The element of millenite is said to normally be found 30 miles below ground and to act as a spiritual conductor.

Are all of the above-mentioned people who claim interdimensional and time travel clinically insane? The answer is "yes." Classic symptoms of paranoid schizophrenia, as defined by clinical psychology, would include such experiences. However, these people are clearly functional despite their unconventional views. Could it actually be that the Damanhur commune members' consciousnesses are tapping into other worlds that affect their astral and/or physical travel to those worlds? What if schizophrenic mental illness is related to a misalignment of the various energy fields that make up the mental and physical human being and result in a person's uncontrolled perception of interpenetrating realities and the inability to distinguish between one time stream and another?

This misalignment of human energy fields can occur spontaneously. For example, the onset of schizophrenia is common during adolescence. There are also reports that this misalignment can occur by accident via high tech interdimensional meddling such as in the classic abduction scenario.

Many abductee accounts testify about the separation of the astral from the physical aspects of the human subject during the process of abduction. The surgical procedures are often conducted in the astral or "Fourth Density" realm, a bandwidth of reality which appears to occur in the "future" relative to the 3D world. Afterwards, the subjects' subtle energy fields are catapulted backwards in time and merged together again with their more dense physical structures. It is not hard to imagine how such procedures, especially if conducted repeatedly on a human being, could result in considerable wear and tear both mentally and physically. There are chilling references to a high incidence of people who have not been properly reassembled by this alien technology and are now crowding our mental institutions. Such interdimensional accidents could help explain the unusual mental state of some conspiracy proponents as well as their debunkers!

Bob Beckwith, a lifelong electrical engineer and author of the book *Hypotheses*, has his own observations about the reports of profound psychological disruption in the sailors who were caught up in what he calls the "Divided Space" energy field of the Philadelphia Experiment. The IX-97 he refers to in the following quote is the ship he knows was involved in such an experiment and that he believes was the actual ship utilized in what he calls the "real" Philadelphia Experiment.

"It may be that the bodies of the sailors on the deck of the IX-97 had become separated into a number of isolated spaces...If so, nerve signals could not flow across the dividing boundaries. It is easy to visualize the disruption of the functioning of a body so divided.

"QUESTION: Is the drastic effect experienced by sailors participating in the Philadelphia Experiment related to conditions of mental patients, in general? Could something be learned from reports of the experiment, if they could be declassified? Surely this 54-year-old information could now be made available to the mental health industry if requested for possible use in the free portion of our scientific community."

Conversely, Beckwith suggests that this same understanding of the entire range of energetics that constitute the nonphysical and physical aspects of a human entity could be used to develop an "insidious, offensive, antipersonnel weapon, leaving little or no trace of its use."

What is particularly noteworthy about Bob Beckwith is that he is a nuts and bolts engineer who relies on hard science in his accounts of the "real" Philadelphia

Experiment. More will be said about his experiences and hard science in the following chapter.

According to widespread conspiracy traditions, the Phoenix Project, which grew out of the Philadelphia Experiment and some of which was carried out at the military base in Montauk, involved tests of the electronic manipulation of human consciousness. According to Preston Nichols and other survivors, the mind control experiments of the Montauk Project were done on individuals as well as on a mass level. The mass mind control experiments were done on the unwitting inhabitants of the hamlet of Montauk as well as on the general population of the Greater New York/Boston megalopolis lying within the 250 mile range of the SAGE antenna on the base.

Rumor has it that the ionospheric tests of the HAARP Project, currently taking place in Alaska, are in actuality the most recent outgrowth of the Phoenix Project. Conspiracy watchers claim that HAARP is picking up where the Montauk Project left off in the testing of means to control specified frequency ranges within the electromagnetic spectrum, from the encryption of military communications to, more significantly, the subordination of human brainwaves worldwide.

A notable property of all waveforms is that of entrainment whereby stronger frequencies cause surrounding weaker frequencies to resonate with them. It is not impossible to envision the deployment of a psychoactive signal that would effect brainwave entrainment on a mass scale. This could possibly be achieved by modulating the resonance fields of the extensive electrical power supply grids already in place around the world. The entire electromagnetic field within the ionospheric shell surrounding the planet could thereby be saturated with psychoactive

THE PHYSICS OF INSANITY

frequencies. This concept is not merely viable. According to Valdamar Valerian, in his seminal conspiracy compendium *Matrix III*, the technology is already very much in use by the Secret Government. True or not, the scenario is not inconceivable from the standpoint of a military looking to develop nonlethal weapons. A "soft" weapon that would eliminate the muss and fuss of real estate damage, make everyone keep going to their jobs, and keep the economy humming would seem worthy of development to a military mentality. Such an operation would arguably be humanitarian and preferable to a nuclear holocaust!

Is this the hidden purpose of the electromagnetic cage created by the thousands of satellites now careening around the Earth that bombard us with frequencies that drive billions of cell phones, satellite TVs, and the wireless Internet? What about the immense barrage of ground-based radio, microwave, and other EM fields leeching out of our refrigerators, computers, and the endless amount of appliances that comprise our daily life and spew out signals that constantly pulse through all of our bodies? It would seem that any paranoia over HAARP is almost a diversion from the fact that we are already sitting ducks in a cancer-causing electronic prison that fuels continuous profits for AMA-approved pharmaceutical industrial products.

There are fascinating contactee accounts from a variety of sources that suggest that the most effective forms of mind control involve electrically imprinting the actual DNA of human beings. Montauk Project survivor Stewart Swerdlow uses the terms "DNA" and "Mind Pattern" interchangeably. He suggests that DNA is a molecular representation of a specific range of consciousness frequencies akin to a circuit board through which the nonphysical aspects of a conscious entity interface with physical reality.

Other alien contactees go a step further and suggest that, from a multidimensional perspective, the human organism is a living holographic projection mechanism through which the experience of three-dimensional reality is created. In other words, the phenomenon popularly known as "physical reality" is projected "outward" from deep within the human soul.

This concept is compellingly congruent with the "observer created reality" theory of Quantum Mechanics. In addition, it dovetails with salient details in the Montauk Project legend whereby the creation of interdimensional vortexes, which enabled travel to the past and future, required the electromagnetic harnessing of a human subject's energy field or soul. Within this paradigm, one could easily see how the power of mass consciousness, and the energetic control thereof, could be of utmost importance to anyone with an interest in maintaining or otherwise affecting the status quo of reality itself.

Contactee reports suggest that reality as we know it is programmable and that higher-dimensional manipulators have the ability to electrically imprint people's DNA and cause them to perceive reality-mimicking artificial holograms. Contactee literature is crammed with claims that many key historical events were just these sorts of holographic inserts. Events which altered the course of human history never "really" happened in a natural manner. It has been said that this alien technology has been perfected over the course of the last 50 years by using the duped military test subjects of the Phoenix Project. There are warnings that a scenario reminiscent of that in the film *The Matrix* could actually occur whereby conventional human reality is replaced with an alien holographic facsimile.

If these reports have any truth to them at all, they offer yet another insight as to how people such as Phil Schneider (as well as others involved in secret government projects) have ended up with their common worldview. Schneider and others who claim to have worked in close proximity with highly-intelligent and apparently highly-manipulative nonhuman entities may have been early test subjects of a sophisticated technology that induced elaborate hallucinations designed to mimic our reality. This technology is said to electrically imprint the human DNA, a technology that some say may eventually be deployed on large population groups.

Talk about the physics of insanity! While it may be of interest to have an awareness of the many horrendous and paranoid machinations mentioned throughout this book, it is clearly unproductive to obsess about such things. Without accepting or rejecting any of the above information outright, it is my opinion that many keys to the puzzle of human existence can be found in the new physics and in the realm of conspiracy legend. Next, we will look at some real experiences and hard physics.

HOME OF THE "REAL" PHILADELPHIA EXPERIMENT?

Above is a photo of the *U.S.S. Martha's Vineyard*, originally a private yacht named *Thelma* which was loaned to the Navy by her owner, George A. Miller, on January 11, 1943. Known also by the classification IX-97, this ship was used as an experimental minesweeper although it was not originally constructed as such. At least one man, Bob Beckwith, believes that the experiments aboard this ship were responsible for the legend of the Philadelphia Experiment.

14

THE "REAL" PHILADELPHIA EXPERIMENT

During the writing of this book, I was introduced to Bob Beckwith, the owner of a successful electrical engineering firm that services utility industries throughout the world. Beckwith is an innovator who has patented many electrical systems over his long career, and he shows no signs of quitting today. He continues to develop and sell electrical protection and control equipment at a time of life when most people are in their second or third decade of retirement.

Late in 1942, while still in his early twenties, Beckwith invented Frequency Shift Keyed transfer trip equipment which facilitated the sending of electrical power over long distances. This was part of a nationally coordinated electric utility crash program to connect existing generation together to supply power to the world's first nuclear facilities such as the one at Hanford in Washington State.

Bob's wunderkind status led to his being tapped by Bell Labs for a project to improve sonar technology. This was urgently needed to defend against the German mines that were being laid off the U.S. coasts and were blowing

Navy boats out of the water before they could reach the European theater.

Beckwith recalls that while the refinement of radar and grappling with its ramifications were of chief importance to wartime electrical engineers on the European front, "Radar was not a major problem to the Navy in the defense of the U.S. coast whereas submarines and the new German mine were." This is an interesting divergence from the predominating accounts of the Philadelphia Experiment legend which usually include a tangent about the Navy's frantic rush to develop "radar invisibility." As Beckwith remembers it, however, the radar war took place mainly in the skies over Europe. According to him, the protection of the U.S. Coast was the primary objective of the "real" Philadelphia Experiment, and it was not a test of radar per se.

Between WW I and WW II, the Germans had developed underwater mines that were set off by the magnetism of passing ships' hulls requiring no direct contact with the targets. The U.S. countered by developing minesweepers that were successful in setting off the German mines with the use of low frequency AC current-carrying cables dragged in the water over the sides, much in the manner of commercial fishing nets. The AC current from the cables activated the mines' detectors thus exploding them at a safe distance. The Germans responded by developing a nasty new mine anchored to the bottom that would not explode when their detectors were activated but would, instead, rise to the surface to get the minesweeper. There were many fatalities and keeping U.S. shipping lanes open became a major problem. The super weapon, the atomic bomb, was not ready yet, and it was feared that the German mine problem might cause the U.S. to lose the war before 'The Bomb' could be used.

As a civilian working for a U.S. Navy contractor, Bell Laboratories, Beckwith was involved in sonar and communications tests over the course of many months. At the time, he was told that Vannevar Bush, the presidential appointee in charge of the Office of Scientific Research and Development, had commissioned his project. Initial tests were carried out in a secret lake in New Jersey. Later, he says tests were carried out in Long Island Sound using the experimental minesweeper IX-97 and the private yacht Sardonix. The Navy's underwater sound lab in New London, Connecticut was also utilized.

It was hoped that an application of Beckwith's Frequency Shift Keyed telemetry technology to sonar would enable the detection of the new mines at a sufficient distance to avoid and/or detonate them safely. While this application of FSK proved unsuccessful, he did help the Navy to develop sonar for communications that was inaudible to the Germans.

There were other ways around the problem of the new German mine that were evidently tested as well. In January of 1943, Beckwith says he attended an initial briefing with the father of the atom bomb, Dr. Edward Teller. Teller described to him a small-scale teleportation demonstration by Nikola Tesla which he intended to duplicate using a full-scale minesweeper.

Eighteen months later, in June of 1944, while Beckwith was running his advanced sonar tests aboard the IX-97, he recalls overhearing the enlisted shipmates' repeated remarks about the apparent results of Teller's secret teleportation project. A very strange series of incidents were reported to have taken place during a previous clandestine experiment aboard the IX-97 in which Beckwith was not personally involved. The details of the stories he continually overheard from his fellow shipmates are strikingly similar to the salient features of the Philadelphia Experiment legend. These highlights included the accidental teleportation of a Navy vessel from Philadelphia to a Naval base in Virginia and the horrible consequence of a sailor's body becoming fused with the ship's hull. Beckwith is convinced that these anecdotes, which he overheard from the crew about the previous experiment aboard the IX-97, were about the "real" Philadelphia Experiment.

In a letter to me, Beckwith writes:

"As I have said in my book, *Hypotheses* (published in 1996), the remarkable time reversal trip of the previous experiment on the IX-97 was common scuttlebutt shared with me at meals, etc. during 'my' experiment. Officers had undoubtedly been told to keep the time travel event secret and were dismayed at the talk going around freely to outsiders such as myself. Remember, there was no CIA or NSA at that time. There were no classifications of secrecy except to not do anything to help the enemy as long as the war continued. It is easy to imagine a small number of high ranking military and political figures organizing a cover story to discredit the scuttlebutt.

"The stories (I constantly overheard) were about the disappearance and movement of the IX-97 and disturbing results that led the skipper and experimenters to quickly shut down the experiment when they suddenly found themselves at the dock in Newport News, VA where the ship had been berthed two weeks previously.

"Navy operators and undoubtedly at least one civilian in charge of the experiment may have been completely enclosed in the inner ships cabin space and 'went along for the ride' with no ill effects. The IX-97 may have stayed in Newport News long enough for those frightened operators of the experiment, enclosed in the space, to see where they were and suddenly turn off the power, bringing the ship back to Philadelphia yards. Unfortunate sailors on deck or the dock must have been partly moved in time giving them the mind disturbing space separation reported.

"One most unfortunate mate fell from the deck to a position where he was trapped in the steelwork. Part of his body was inside and part outside of a splash cowling just forward of a port side cabin's sliding door. I was shown fresh paint on the inside and outside of this curved cowling where the mate had been impaled, half in and half out of the cabin.

"I clearly remember the scuttlebutt among those of us working together in New London concerning the experiments and I had no reason not to believe the stories which included the man trapped in steelwork and men with very serious mental disorders. One mate was said to have later faded from plain sight in a barroom, never to appear again! The mealtime and free time conversations may or may not have included Dr. Horton (the director of Beckwith's subsequent sonar project), but I believe some did. As to the validity of the scuttlebutt concerning the ship moving experiment, I can only say that jokes of this kind simply were not made up during the war. Besides, how could one hoax a story involving so many people?"

Beckwith's testimony is a very interesting and exciting development in the unraveling of this World War II secret. Conspicuously absent from this version of the Philadelphia Experiment are the figures of John von Neumann, "Dr. Rinehart" and the *USS Eldridge* which are all normally associated with the legend. Beckwith is convinced that these details are part of the disinformational campaign set up by the Navy to confuse the issue and discredit accounts of what actually took place. For their part, the Navy has put some effort into denying that anything like the Philadelphia Experiment ever took place. In fact, they seem to do a brisk business substantiating their side of the story by selling copies of the microfilm of the *Eldridge's* logbook from their website (number NRS-1978-26, if you are interested).

As to verifying Beckwith's claims, I have seen a copy of a photo ID civilian pass the Navy issued to him in May of 1944 which gave him access to government and military facilities, boats, and submarines. I have also seen his numerous expense reports. In the Navy's official *Dictionary of American Fighting Ships* by Samuel Eliot Morison, there is a photograph and description of the IX-97's activities which document the ship's use in sonar tests in the Long Island Sound area during the time period Beckwith specifies. According to this record, the IX-97 was originally a private yacht named *Thelma* which was loaned to the Navy by her owner, George A. Miller, on January 11, 1943. The "IX" hull classification is for "miscellaneous boats" which explains how it was being used as an experimental minesweeper although it was not originally constructed as such. The Navy rechristened her the *USS Martha's Vineyard,* and she was commissioned on March 30, 1943 with Lt. William W. Boyton in command. On April 18, 1946, she was decommissioned, stripped of military equipment, and returned to her owner.

I asked Beckwith if the name Boyton rang a bell. He said that it did and that it was likely that Boyton was in command of the ship during the teleportation experiment which he estimates having occurred sometime around September and October of 1943. There is no mention of the IX-97 ever traveling to Philadelphia or Newport News in the brief official report that I saw. One way to verify the IX-97's whereabouts would be to access the ship's logs, assuming they are still on file, at the National Archives in Maryland. It should be noted that there was a massive fire in the archives in the 1970's which destroyed many of the Navy's records.

I showed Beckwith the four handwritten Philadelphia Experiment documents attributed to Oscar Schneider. He believes these letters to be genuine Navy documents written by Oscar Schneider but that they were generated as part of the above-mentioned cover-up. To him, the fact that they are handwritten does not make them appear spurious. In his experience, handwritten documents, especially of highly classified information, were not unusual during that era.

In another letter to me, he says:

"My first meeting before the experiment was with Dr. Edward Teller. He had been assigned to the anti-sonar project by the President. Dr. Teller told of an experiment done by Tesla in 1907 where Tesla moved an object along a laboratory bench, turned on his electric field, making the object move back in time to its original position. When the power was turned off, the object moved forward, to its place in present time. If anyone can research Tesla's work and confirm this experiment, it would greatly support this story and my memory.

"Teller said he had no time to repeat Telsa's work and had to believe it would work when scaled up to the size of an experimental minesweeper, the IX-97. The plan was to add a third current-carrying conductor high in the rigging of the boat, forming a three-phase field. High-current rotating generators manufactured by GE at the Pittsfield, Massachusetts plant supplied the three currents. Again, an excellent source of confirming facts, if anyone can find such generators in the General Electric Co. records..."

Beckwith saw these "time travel" generators located at the rear of the craft. Although they were not in use during his tests, they were still onboard. They consisted of three single-phase units placed 120 electrical degrees apart. Each unit was approximately 5' tall by 2' in diameter. The generators put out low voltage but did more than 1000 Amps. He said the boat had sliding doors (which looks right from the picture) and that the controls for the generators were in the back cabin. The generators were electrically driven by the ship's power.

The proposition of Beckwith's "real" Philadelphia Experiment aboard the IX-97 had nothing whatsoever to do with radar invisibility. It was actually an elaboration of Nikola Tesla's earlier work in teleportation.

Teleportation is tantamount to time travel. The idea that the Philadelphia Experiment intentionally involved the manipulation of space-time physics is more congruent with the subsequent legends of the ship's disappearance "from this reality" than the idea of it having been a test of radar invisibility or "cloaking."

15

DIVIDED SPACE

Beckwith conjectures that the premise of Teller's IX-97 test was to teleport the minesweeper to a previous point in its space-time trajectory by encapsulating the boat in a highly specialized three-phase "electromagnetic bottle." As incredible as it sounds, this would allow a ship to "blip" out of the way of a mine to safety. He proposes that the experiment's intent was to give a U.S. vessel, at the flip of a switch, the instantaneous ability to be physically removed from the universal space-time coordinate in which it detected the presence of an enemy mine. Beckwith suggests that the creation of such a separated space-time field can be done by engaging the principles of what he calls 'divided space'.

In his book, *Hypotheses*, Beckwith develops a series of fascinating postulates based on some premises which I will grossly oversimplify here. All atoms in universal space are energetically connected by what are called "strong nuclear force lines" which literally hold the universe together and function as a medium for the transmission of all frequencies. These lines of strong nuclear force can be broken with the application of what is called "a three-phase neutrino field" which, in turn, creates a bubble of "divided space." Beckwith explains that a related phenomenon, which occurs haphazardly in nature, is "ball lightning." Interestingly enough, such ball lightning or "Tesla balls" have figured repeatedly in UFO eyewitness accounts, a detail that will become more meaningful by the end of this chapter.

Beckwith contends that the means of intentionally disrupting these strong force lines is via the manipulation of neutrino fields. Neutrinos interpenetrate all matter in the cosmos. They are the smallest subatomic particles yet measured. Stars are constantly creating new neutrinos which speed throughout the universe in all directions as they become modulated by and carry information about the bodies through which they pass unhindered. As these tiny neutral particles are possibly massless and have an incredibly weak nuclear force, they rarely have an impact on the matter that they pervade. Telescopes to measure neutrinos are constructed beneath huge granite mountains in order to reduce background radiation signals which would hide their very weak signal. It is Beckwith's view that neutrinos have an infinite information handling bandwidth and function as the voice and the power of the universe.

As this information relates to a Philadelphia-type Experiment, he explains:

"A space divided from universal space can be created by causing a small percentage of neutrinos passing through the space to travel in a vortex rotating at a frequency in the order of 7.5 Hertz. Strong force lines at the boundaries of the space are interrupted so long as the vortex exists. This twisting field is necessary to break the field of strong force lines between all matter in universal space and to create an inner space separated from universal space.

"If a rotating magnetic field is operated in synchronism with the Earth's 7.32 Hz fundamental resonance*, objects within one such space can be moved with respect to our 'universal space' when power is applied. The divided space is then free of forces of inertia or gravity. Once the space is divided, objects within the space may levitate, teleport, or move in time. Divided inner space can pass through universal space but is dependent on the drag and surface sharpness between spaces being low enough to prevent piercing the shell of the missing strong force lines. Electromagnetic waves, including visible light and infra red heat can pass through the boundaries of the divided spaces."

As to how these hypotheses apply to his recollection of the minesweeper's layout and how this teleportation experiment played out, he says:

"The forward cabin formed the research room housing our experimental gear. The bridge was above us. A second cabin towards the stern housed three special looking generators, motor-driven from ship's power. Controls for these generators were also housed in the second cabin.

"I believe three phase currents were placed through the wires at a low frequency. This frequency was most likely the 7.32 Hz fundamental

---

* While several New Age publications have claimed that the Earth's resonance has sped up to 13.5 Hz or 21 Hz, Beckwith disagrees and points out that these higher frequencies are harmonics of the fundamental resonance of 7.32 Hz.

frequency recognized by Tesla and first measured by Jack Shulman.

"As they gradually eased the power up, the experimenters found that lower power levels had no noticeable effect. Suddenly, a frequency threshold was crossed and wham, they traveled back two weeks in time instead of the desired 15 minutes or so needed to get out of the way of a mine. Once separated, the inner space containing the ship apparently moved back to a time when the ship was berthed at Newport News, VA.

"As the current level in the three cables was increased, force lines began to tear between the ship and universal space. Only when the level reached the point that all the lines were broken, was the IX-97 free from the pull of the earth and the time of the present.

"The boat was free to suddenly go wherever it is that things within a divided space go. In the case of the IX-97, that place was two weeks back in time to the place where it was at berth in Newport News. Turning off the power when the skipper saw what had happened reconnected the divided space to universal space, jerking the boat back to the Philadelphia Navy yard harbor. The return of the IX-97 to Philadelphia was within seconds of the time it left, not in 1984, as in the science fiction version released to movie houses in 1984...

"More sophisticated equipment may have been involved in preparing the minesweeper than that described here. I had the sense of a quick experiment gotten together in a matter of a few months and must have been rather simple addition to the 'standard' minesweeper. Since we needed all the

162

minesweepers we could get into active service, it surely was the IX-97 that made the time trip and was kept out of duty a few months longer for our subsequent experiment with FM/SSB communications in 1944.

"It appears that the Philadelphia Experiment [with the IX-97] was planned in part at least, by Dr. Horton and others at Bell Labs and people at the underwater sound lab [at the New London, CT Naval base] that we worked with in the subsequent communications experiment. The IX-97 must have been the minesweeper involved since what other reason would there have been for the third overhead 'degaussing' cable?

"The [Philadelphia] experiment could well have been planned and carried out by civilian scientists with little involvement of the Navy, as with the work in which I was involved.

"Retired Army Intelligence officer, Col. Phillip J. Corso has confirmed the experiment from work he did with Admiral Burke while Chairman and chief policy maker of President Eisenhower's National Security Administration. Corso tells me (Bob Beckwith) of Burke's knowledge of the experiment and his deep concern and his regret over the loss of life that resulted. Corso tells me that my recall of the event has greater detail than any other source that he knows of. He tells me that the project continued and has progressed greatly since then. Col. Corso has kindly given permission to use his name for this important confirmation of my 55 year old memory."

One year after Beckwith self-published *Hypotheses,* Phillip Corso released his book *The Day After Roswell.* Corso received considerable publicity and his book ended up on the *New York Times* best-seller list. This was unheard-of at the time for a book alleging that such things as fiber optics and laser discs are actually back-engineered alien technology obtained from the U.S. military's interaction with the infamous Greys. Not surprisingly, Corso was dead within a year of the book's release.

While Beckwith is convinced that the *Eldridge* legend is the Navy's disinformational fabrication, I do not see how his IX-97 story disproves it. If the principles of divided space that he describes are viable, they would surely have been tested more than once and on more than one vessel. God only knows where the evolution of that technology would have led to by now.

Actually, Beckwith does have an idea of one way this technology is being applied by the Navy today. He has sent me a 46 page commemorative booklet on the *U.S.S. Cardinal,* a modern day minesweeper which he recently toured. The vessel is one of ten or so "Osprey class" ships completed over the past decade. According to the Navy's own brochure on the *Cardinal,* "The ships' hulls are a solid, continuous monocoque structure laminated from special fiberglass and resin. They are easy to maintain and flex to absorb the violent shock of an underwater mine explosion. The ships are designed to have very low magnetic and acoustic signatures, giving them an added margin of safety during operations." This description seems to suggest that the ship's laminate is related to the coating on Stealth Fighters and that it is apparently the state-of-the-art in "radar invisibility." The officer leading the tour told him that there is no iron of any kind allowed on the ship, not even paperclips.

U.S.S. CARDINAL

Above is a photo of the *U.S.S. Cardinal*, one of the Navy's special
"Osprey class" of ships believed to utilize time technology.

Beckwith believes that this "fiberglass" construction
is made of Carbon 14 which he says is "10,000 stronger
than normal Carbon 12 diamonds and is also a supercon-
ductor over a wide temperature range." During his lecture
tour of the minesweeper, he was told that duty on Osprey
class vessels such as the *Cardinal* is among the most
sought after in the Navy. Already, the fleet has cleared the
Earth's coasts of mines, and they are keeping ahead of
those laying more.

He says that he saw the modern version of the three-
phase divided space generators aboard the *Cardinal* and
described them as being the size of "extra wide refrigerators." The units are produced by MATRA-Marconi, a
European consortium that is a leader in satellite technology and is now apparently defense contracting for the U.S.
Navy. Interestingly, MATRA-Marconi, whose namesake
was a bitter rival of Tesla's, has been awarded a contract
for a mission to Mars in 2003.

Beckwith is convinced that the class of minesweeper to which the *Cardinal* belongs has the "ability to bop around the world thus extending the ability of the IX-97 by 60 years." In other words, the superconducting hulls confer controlled teleportation capabilities to the ships. In addition, he believes that these Osprey class boats have the ability to generate a field around them which keeps them one second ahead of the universal space timeline; thereby enabling them to evade detection of any kind. A crew member told him that the men hate whenever they have to salvage enemy mines and get on deck in order to do so because that is the only time they can ever be seen. Otherwise, if the men are within the field of the ship's cabin, they, along with the entire vessel, are completely invisible.

In a letter to me, he writes:

"In a one-on-one discussion with the mission control officer, I was told that the only way one knew where one of the Osprey Class ships were was to look at a display map of about one mile diameter having a boat icon showing their position. He said that this display would change instantly from Tampa to the Persian Gulf, just like it did in simulator training. The day after leaving Tampa, they would be working at a site in Japan. The crew doesn't try very hard to keep their secret, depending instead on the experience that the secret is safe simply because no one will ever believe the truth."

It is also interesting to note that Phillip Corso, one of the founding members of the NSA, personally told Beckwith that a related secret project to that of the IX-97 had "progressed greatly" since the 1940's. The implications of this are mind-boggling. Was it an oblique reference to these Osprey class ships or even to the Montauk Project? Could an entire underground base be constructed and maintained within the field of a divided space within a "bubble" reality that is slightly out of phase with and imperceptible from the perspective of everyday universal space? Does the military today possess aircraft that have onboard generators which create these three-phase divided space fields? If so, could the extremely fast 45 degree angle turning UFOs reported worldwide actually be the witnessed maneuvers of super high-tech human military craft? Could the "Tesla balls" reported in the vicinity of UFOs be "droplets" of the divided space energy field that have dripped off of aircraft equipped with these generators?

Beckwith's extraordinary information is particularly jarring because of his deadpan "nuts-and-bolts" delivery as an engineer. In the next chapter, written by Peter Moon, we will have a look at another "nuts and bolts" researcher who has delivered incontrovertible proof that there has been a concerted effort by the Navy to cover up the research which is now known in common lore as the Philadelphia Experiment.

16

COVER-UP

(Note: This chapter is written by Peter Moon)
Those of you who have scoured the Internet for information about the Philadelphia Experiment will be familiar with the name of Marshall Barnes, a researcher who has sought to prove beyond the shadow of a doubt that the Navy lied about the Philadelphia Experiment and that there has been a massive cover up of what happened.

In the early 1990's, Marshall had stumbled across the information circulated by Joe Matheny on Ong's Hat and began to seriously study parallel universes and quantum physics. He had also studied John von Neumann, the man believed to be responsible for the Montauk time technology. When he read *The Montauk Project*, he was intrigued by the fact that Preston Nichols knew things about John von Neumann that completely aligned with his research.

Many years ago, I received a phone call from a writer at *Fate* magazine who wanted a copy of one my books. I complained to him that they never review our books so why should I send him a book. He then told me that the problem with our books is that they have no credibility. Well then, why did he want them? I then pointed out to him that there is obvious documentation as far as a secret project having taken place. Of course, everyone knows that the more sensational details of the Montauk Project legend are not fully provable at this point. As I pressed him and told him that I had information indicating his magazine has produced deliberate false information about the Philadelphia Experiment, he finally admitted that he wanted the books because he was personally interested in the subject matter. As he has a family to feed, he did not want to take up the cause against his editors. I told him I understood and sent him a book. This poor man was apparently under oppressive editorial dictates from a publication that prides itself on promoting paranormal and "far out" information but seems to play down the real questions with regard to understanding the truth.

The above example is reflective of a mentality that seeks to dismiss the information regarding the Philadelphia Experiment by means of knocking its credibility. These type of people fail to zero in on the exact nature of the problem: concealed information and hidden truth. "Knocking the credibility" serves as a hapless and poor excuse for applying yourself to the task of finding or seeing the truth.

I was alerted to the above problems with *Fate* by Philadelphia Experiment researcher Marshall Barnes when he wrote an article for *The Montauk Pulse* in the Spring 1997 edition. In this article, Marshall brought up the case of a man who called himself "Drue" and claimed to be a survivor of the Philadelphia Experiment. For those of you who are not familiar with "Drue," he became a short-lived celebrity on the Philadelphia Experiment circuit by making outrageous claims. In his writings and in his video taped presentation to the 1996 Global Sciences Conference, Drue claimed that according to the February 1996 issue of *Scientific American*, IBM had the ability to teleport objects from one spot to another and that he had worked with them. This was not true, and Marshall could prove it. IBM had made claims that were somewhat similar but they were not so exotic. Drue went further by saying that the idea of melting crayons was an example of the effect created by the Philadelphia Experiment. Of course, if this were true, no rematerialization of any kind would be possible. Most remarkable of all were his claims that the *Eldridge* appeared at Lake Mead, a location hours away from his home in California. To accompany his theory, he took people out on "tours" to feel the vibrations of what had happened. Drue obviously had no scientific training and his explanations made anyone with any real knowledge of science cringe. Marshall pointed out in his article that Drue was a disinformation artist because *nothing* he said about the Philadelphia Experiment was true. Despite the above, Drue was met with open arms by many media outlets that included *Fate* magazine and different nationally syndicated television and radio shows. Up to this time, Preston Nichols has been comparatively ignored by such media. The only apparent explanation for this could be an organized disinformation campaign calculated to kill the Philadelphia Experiment story. Marshall concluded that the conspirators wanted someone spurious to represent the Philadelphia Experiment. That way, no one could believe a word of it.

According to Marhsall's research, another character was enlisted to help discredit the legends and stories ascribed to the Philadelphia Experiment. This was famous author Jacques Vallee who, in the "prestigious" *Journal of Scientific Exploration,* wrote an article entitled "Anatomy of a Hoax." Vallee is a very well known researcher in the UFO community who has prided himself on having an open mind to UFOs and similar subjects. By taking such an open mind, he has won the heart of many UFO enthusiasts. Vallee based his article on someone who claimed to be an actual witness to the event which has been labeled as the Philadelphia Experiment. This expose of the Philadelphia Experiment being a "hoax" was hailed by prominent UFO researchers as the best research yet on the subject. Marshall Barnes did some background digging on the witness, a "Mr. Dudgeon," and established that the witness was lying. Navy documents and historical information indicated that Mr. Dudgeon could not have possibly witnessed the experiment on its alleged dates and that his statements to Vallee were false as well. Additionally, Marshall dug up admissions from Vallee himself that he had been taught to write disinformation. To compound the situation, Marshall also linked Vallee to being a member of the "Aviary," a group of former CIA and other agents who are dedicated to studying, infiltrating, and disinforming the UFO community.

Marshall did not stop there. He sent an eight page report to the editor of the *Journal of Scientific Exploration*, Bernard Haisch, and informed him of all the evidence he had acquired as well as his intention to expose Vallee as a deliberate fraud. Instead of informing his reading audience of Marshall's condemning evidence, Haisch wanted to know if Marshall was going to put the information on the Internet. This defensive posture by Haisch was viewed as an attempt to cover up the full truth about the Philadelphia Experiment.

Things got even more strange when I received a phone call from Mark Caras, a producer for Towers Productions who said he wanted to interview people about the Philadelphia Experiment. They were doing a show to be aired on the A&E channel. I gave him the phone numbers of Preston Nichols, Al Bielek, and Marshall

Barnes. Caras swore he was on the up and up and that he was going to do a real and honest production. Although he sounded sincere, I know the media well enough to know they can seldom be trusted. I declined to be interviewed under any circumstances.

Mark Caras seemed to hit it off with Marshall and began to get involved in the investigation a bit himself. According to Marshall, he called Bernard Haisch and indicated they were considering including the article "Anatomy of a Hoax" in their television documentary. Subsequently, Caras reported that Haisch was unnerved by Marshall's call and was nervous about an episode being done on the hoax article. Caras also called Jacques Vallee but received no reply. Finally, he left a message indicating that he was going to proceed with an episode featuring Marshall's statements without any rebuttal by Vallee. Calling back within five minutes of the message, Vallee was quoted as saying that he was "sorry that he had anything to do with the Philadelphia Experiment" and was worried about his reputation in the UFO and venture capital communities as a result of Marshall's investigation. Marshall was about to strike at Vallee's disinformation by releasing true information and blasting it across the Internet and through other channels. Instead, he waited for Caras to do an interview with Vallee in hopes that the latter would be caught off guard.

Things took another twist when Marshall was to be taped for his interview in Caras' production. He was handed a release form that seemed to stray away from the prior agreement he had with Caras. As it was a standard release form and as Caras assured him that he would honor their prior agreement, Marshall signed the form giving them freedom to edit as they pleased. During the subsequent shooting, Marshall demonstrated his main thesis that proves the Navy had the data and resources to experiment with invisibility in 1943.

While Bob Beckwith has claimed the Philadelphia Experiment had to with Telsa's early teleportation experiments and others have claimed the issue was radar, Marshall Barnes has brought up another issue: optical invisibility. In his own research, he arrived at the conclusion that an intense electromagnetic field could create a mirage effect of invisibility by refracting light. Although this originally came from "Dr. Rinehart" in William Moore's book *The Philadelphia Experiment: Project Invisibility*, there was no full explanation given in that work. Marshall verified the scientific possibility of such a mirage effect in a college text book entitled *Physics: Volume 2* (by Richard Wilson and Jay M. Fasachoff). The actual cover of the text book shows a particle accelerator device in water that is surrounded by a greenish-bluish glow, the same glow that was noted around the *Eldridge* in eyewitness accounts. What is interesting is that the college text book describes the glow to be the result of dielectric breakdown of the air near the surface of the water. "Dielectric breakdown" is the very same term Dr. Rinehart used in the aforementioned book. This was just one fact that demonstrated not only that there was scientific plausibility behind the Philadelphia Experiment but that the Navy had the means and research capabilities to address such an issue. There are more details to this which you can view on the Internet. The main point here is that an orchestrated cover-up was being perpetrated.

To demonstrate the plausibility of invisibility, Marshall Barnes found a special plastic called "diffraction film" which refracts light. When you place the film in front of an object, you can "see through" the object. It demonstrates that invisibility is a relatively easy way to camouflage an object. Of course, there are more scientific implications when one considers the broad electromagnetic spectrum, but Marshall was trying to prove a simple point: the Office of Naval Research had lied in their publicity release about the Philadelphia Experiment when they indicated they did not have the scientific capability to perform such an operation.

All of the above, and in much more detail, was included in Marhsall's interview for Mark Caras and Towers Productions. Marshall even included a video wherein the diffraction film could be used to make a ship appear invisible. The actual ship was an actual size replica of Columbus' ship the *Santa Maria*. Finally, and at long last, irrefutable evidence would be supplied that the Navy had lied about the experiment and it was going to appear on national television. Hopefully, this would start a renaissance in scientific and government disclosure.

Much to everyone's dismay, the show did air but not with any of the above relevant information. Preston Nichols, who was interviewed, did not appear either. The show that did air was "The Unexplained" and was a mockery of the truth. Caras had already warned Marshall that the producer, Jonathan Towers, had ordered changes in the script. Next, there would be no time to cover the Jacques Valles issue. Instead, "The Unexplained" show featured an official U.S. naval historian who said, as far as he knew, the Navy never experimented with making ships invisible with magnetic fields.

Additionally, the show featured Robert Goerman, a writer who had actually met Carlos Allende's family through coincidence. He wrote an article for *Fate* magazine in 1980 entitled "Alias: Carlos Allende." Goerman, as did his article, portrayed Carlos as a giant "leg-puller" who showed signs of great intelligence but never fully

PHILADELPHIA EXPERIMENT MURDER

Return to Naval Historical Center home page. Return to Frequently Asked Questions page.

DEPARTMENT OF THE NAVY – NAVAL HISTORICAL CENTER
901 M STREET SE – WASHINGTON NAVY YARD
WASHINGTON DC 20374-5060

Related resources:: Philadelphia Experiment

DEPARTMENT OF THE NAVY
OFFICE OF NAVAL RESEARCH
ARLINGTON, VIRGINIA 22217

Information Sheet: Philadelphia Experiment

Over the years, the Navy has received innumerable queries about the so-called "Philadelphia Experiment" or "Project" and the alleged role of the Office of Naval Research (ONR) in it. The majority of these inquiries are directed to the Office of Naval Research or to the Fourth Naval District in Philadelphia. The frequency of these queries predictably intensifies each time the experiment is mentioned by the popular press, often in a science fiction book.

The genesis of the Philadelphia Experiment myth dates back to 1955 with the publication of *The Case for UFO's* by the late Morris K. Jessup.

Some time after the publication of the book, Jessup received correspondence from a Carlos Miquel Allende, who gave his address as R.D. #1, Box 223, New Kensington, Pa. In his correspondence, Allende commented on Jessup's book and gave details of an alleged secret naval experiment conducted by the Navy in Philadelphia in 1943. During the experiment, according to Allende, a ship was rendered invisible and teleported to and from Norfolk in a few minutes, with some terrible after-effects for crew members. Supposedly, this incredible feat was accomplished by applying Einstein's "unified field" theory. Allende claimed that he had witnessed the experiment from another ship and that the incident was reported in a Philadelphia newspaper. The identity of the newspaper has never been established. Similarly, the identity of Allende is unknown, and no information exists on his present address.

In 1956 a copy of Jessup's book was mailed anonymously to ONR. The pages of the book were interspersed with hand-written comments which alleged a knowledge of UFO's, their means of motion, the culture and ethos of the beings occupying these UFO's, described in pseudo-scientific and incoherent terms.

Two officers, then assigned to ONR, took a personal interest in the book and showed it to Jessup. Jessup concluded that the writer of those comments on his book was the same person who had written

OFFICIAL NAVY RESPONSE

Above and on the following page is an account by the Navy of the Philadelphia Experiment legend and how it came into being. The last statement says that "ONR has never conducted any investigations on invisibility, either in 1943 or at any other time." Marshall Barnes knows that invisibility was investigated by the Navy and that it was not a stretch of existing scientific knowledge at all.

him about the Philadelphia Experiment. These two officers personally had the book retyped and arranged for the reprint, in typewritten form, of 25 copies. The officers and their personal belongings have left ONR many years ago, and ONR does not have a file copy of the annotated book.

Personnel at the Fourth Naval District believe that the questions surrounding the so-called "Philadelphia Experiment" arise from quite routine research which occurred during World War II at the Philadelphia Naval Shipyard. Until recently, it was believed that the foundation for the apocryphal stories arose from degaussing experiments which have the effect of making a ship undetectable or "invisible" to magnetic mines. Another likely genesis of the bizarre stories about levitation, teleportation and effects on human crew members might be attributed to experiments with the generating plant of a destroyer, the USS Timmerman. In the 1950's this ship was part of an experiment to test the effects of a small, high-frequency generator providing 1,000 hz instead of the standard 400hz. The higher frequency generator produced corona discharges, and other well known phenomena associated with high frequency generators. None of the crew suffered effects from the experiment.

ONR has never conducted any investigations on invisibility, either in 1943 or at any other time (ONR was established in 1946.) In view of present scientific knowledge, ONR scientists do not believe that such an experiment could be possible except in the realm of science fiction.

08 September 1996

lived up to his potential and was too scattered to accomplish much.

Although Goerman stumbled across the truth, he did not seem to have any recognition of some very relevant facts. His article indicates that Carl or Carlos used to send many copies of his data, often with his famous multicolored pen notations, to family members for safekeeping. It was as if he was trying to secure the information for posterity. This behavior is not the action of a simple "legpuller." It sounds much more like someone who is obsessed with preserving the truth. What is more remarkable is that, according to the article, the family reveals that Carlos one time orchestrated a fake cardiac arrest. What is interesting about the specific circumstances revealed is that he had demonstrated remarkable knowledge that only a trained physician would ordinarily know. When I read the article, it seemed to me that Goerman had completely missed the point. Carlos Allende was a genius. Not only did he possess remarkable insight to physics but to the subject of medicine as well. He is indeed a candidate for being intimately involved in the Philadelphia Experiment.

During his interview, Goerman had the audacity to say that other researchers, who decried his article, ignored his findings because they wanted to sell their books. The program then cut to Marhsall in a defamatory manner as if he was one of the "other researchers." Ultimately, "The Unexplained" summed up their findings for the show with a quote: "To this day, there are no credible documents or witnesses to support the Philadelphia Experiment."

Caras had dishonored his verbal agreement with Marshall who felt lied to and violated. He was set up to look like a fool and his factual hard earned evidence was ignored. Marshall also knew that Caras was well aware of his research and the truth. In fact, Marshall even got copies of the invoices which showed that Caras had purchased diffraction film for purposes of the production. To Marshall, all of this smacked of being an intelligence operation from the very beginning.

Marshall followed up these atrocities by calling up John Reilly, the man who had appeared as an official historian for the Navy. In a taped conversation, Reilly admitted that his clearance was "Secret" and that anything "Top Secret" would be out of his knowledge. Obviously, anything to do with the Philadelphia Experiment would have been "Top Secret." In this manner, John Reilly and the Navy's credibility was completely out the window.

When Marshall called Goerman, he asked if he had written his article on Allende before or after he read the book by William Moore. Goerman said that he had first read the book and then written the article. Asked by Marshall if he checked out the information in the book about Rinehart, Goerman said, "no." In fact, he said that he felt Allende had made up the whole thing about the Philadelphia Experiment and that there was no need to investigate the matter any further. Marshall quoted him as saying, "If Allende made it all up, I don't see what Rinehart has to do with any of it." Obviously, the data offered by Rinehart in the book, as demonstrated by Marshall Barnes, was on the money. Therefore, Allende could not have made up the whole thing.

All of the above demonstrates beyond any shadow of a doubt that there has been a massive effort to "murder" the Philadelphia Experiment story.

Despite his enthusiasm for proving that the Philadelphia Experiment occurred, Marshall Barnes was not convinced at all by the Oscar Schneider documents. They looked like disinformation to him. When Alexandra Bruce faxed him the documents and asked for his analysis, it was as follows (see Chapter 2 for the actual documents):

"My current opinion is that these documents are fake as three dollar bills. For starters, there is no classification called "ABOVE SECRET". There's RESTRICTED, CONFIDENTIAL, SECRET and TOP SECRET. Sometimes ABOVE TOP SECRET is used but that's rare. The letter to Twining makes no sense. Why would they be looking for the DE-173 in 1953 when it had already been sold to the Greeks? The *USS Farunseth* was never in the Philly Naval Yard. It was the "Furuseth" anyway. "Farunseth" is really a fake indicator.

If you've seen handwriting samples, then I would have to say that regardless of who wrote them, they don't make any sense. I also have looked at many documents from that time period and I can't ever remember seeing any that were handwritten. These include letters from Einstein, FDR, Vannevar Bush, and others.

"I have seen communications between military at that time and maybe only one was all handwritten. The rest were typed. I can't imagine (though I could be wrong) something of this magnitude being handled like that. Especially to Twining. It also addresses Twining as a Lieutenant General. Twining went from Lieutenant General to full General in 1950, a full three years before that O. Schneider letter was written. Why would O. Schneider be writing to him as a Lieutenant General in 1953?

"The reason why the Twining data was in that letter is because Twining is implicated in the UFO mystery field. He's famous for a comment he made while a Major General (I believe); that UFOs weren't Air Force experiments. He might also be named in the MJ-12 papers, which I think may also be fake, though I would not say so definitively. I will say that these Schneider papers are definitely fake because there's nothing credible about them: major typos and wrong names, letters addressed to high-ranking officers with their ranks wrong. The whole mess stinks. But if you want to make something look like more than it is, making Twining look like he was a part of this somehow would work because someone investigating it might say, 'Oh, that makes sense because he was part of MJ-12!'

"I'm further convinced that they're fake because it mentions "Reno". It is most probably a reference to a Dr. Franklin Reno, the scientist that worked on the P.E. who talked to Carlos Allende. The big problem here is that that wasn't his real name. It was a pseudonym because the scientist probably had taken an oath of secrecy, like the scientist that I have in my new book, who Moore called "Dr. Rinehart", after the character in the book, *Thin Air*.

"The other problem is that Reno wasn't the real brains behind it, he just helped with some of the equations, so Schneider wouldn't be calling him Reno and he wouldn't really need his "work" anyway. I have extensively researched Reno/ Rinehart and have gotten enough evidence to prove he was most probably real and I can probably find out who he really was.

"There's nothing in these papers so far that impresses me and everything I've found points to them being fake. I know that the August 12th date was fake now too, at least in this timeline. The *Eldridge* was in the harbor by the end of July 1943 for the crew to get on. I know because I've talked to them! The P.E. was done in July. The Eldridge was launched in New Jersey and then they snuck it down to Philly. I've got crew tapes to prove it, which also blows a hole in these Schneider papers because he refers to "its original crew" in the same letter that mentions Reno. Rinehart, Bielek, and I all agree that it wasn't the original crew that was used, unless Schneider is using the wrong terminology. The original crew would have been the ones assigned first. In fact, there's a term called "plank member", which means that the person was there when it was first finished and launched. The men in the P.E. were just test subjects or a test crew. Rinehart even said where some of them came from, which blew me away because it correlated with other research that I had already done and fit perfectly with historical records and even psychological motivation.

"So far, this Schneider stuff looks like a crude attempt at a clever ruse, or a clever attempt to make a crude ruse look clever. On the surface they seem like they really mean something, but under scrutiny they start falling apart. This is like a cheap version of the MJ-12 papers.

"I have completed my analysis. There is absolutely nothing here so far that convinces me that these are genuine. Maybe I wouldn't be so harsh a year ago but I've seen a lot more military documents and talked with a lot more military people and these things have the earmarks of a fraud. Besides, if he had written these things to other people, why the hell did he still have them? If he had sent them they would be in files somewhere so that people like me couldn't find them.

"I think these papers are another way to throw researchers off the track because under scrutiny they could be seen as fakes and then hurt the story all over again. This kind of thing goes on in the UFO field all the time. That's the way I see these Schneider papers functioning.

"I am convinced that Oscar Schneider was involved in high level stuff. Not the Philadelphia Experiment, but perhaps Project Rainbow. What do I mean? Simply this: I found a listing for a final report on a Project Rainbow in some Naval records that was from the '50s. It appears to have been related to radiation effects on optical systems. That's all I know about it. I think it was from around the time of Crossroads, but I'll have to check. I know that the name Project Rainbow was used again later as the code name for the CIA project to lower the U2 spy plane's radar cross section. That there was a Project Rainbow before that had a final report done in the 50s could be related to a final report on what happened in '43 but I'm just speculating, here. It's still a clue."

Although Marshall has brought up some excellent points in his analysis of the documents, it must be realized that he has not served in the military or in military intelligence. Others have claimed him to be involved in such, but he has not come forward with any such claims. Bob Beckwith, who was involved in top secret projects during the war, said that handwritten documents were quite common.

When Alexandra Bruce forwarded Marshall's analysis to Phil Schneider's ex-wife, Cynthia, she "knew better" than to agree with Marshall's opinions. The following information on the next page was her reply.

"I can tell you this: if the letters are fraudulent, then Oscar produced them himself. I saw the original envelopes with the original stamps. The pages were yellow with age. These were not "current" copies made by someone today. These were original documents made decades ago. There may be "mistakes" (or what seems like mistakes) but they are mistakes that Philip would NOT have made.

"A friend of mine had these letters analyzed, and he states that many of the codes are STILL TOP SECRET TODAY, that they are accurate. He actually sounded scared, because by discovering that many of these codes are top secret today, he realized that the information he was holding was correct and possibly 'deadly' in his hands."

Whether the documents are true or not is not the point. Enough evidence has thus far been presented in this book to establish that an elaborate cover up has permeated the Philadelphia Experiment. It is almost made to be a constant conundrum so that it is impossible to figure out.

In the beginning, there was Carlos Allende and his blatant references to mind control. For a further look at the mind control angle and its debris, I will hand you back over to Alexandra Bruce.

17

ATLANTIS

Many ex-intelligence-related proponents of the New World Order theory claim to have highly developed extrasensory abilities which is the reason, they allege, that they came to be employed by the Black Projects to begin with. In the history of each and every one, you will find an experience with mind control. Carlos Allende was the first mind-control candidate to come forth. Even if much of what he said is either wrong or confusing, the man has had a definite impact on the way humanity now looks at itself and at its governments. Therefore, one must not throw the baby out with the bath water when it comes to such individuals. It is more fruitful to sift through the information, see what rings true, and investigate further.

As was discussed earlier, Glen Pruitt and his family were deeply enmeshed in secret government projects and mind control. If one searches the hard-facts angle with regard to this family, one will follow a trail so labyrinthine that it could not possibly have been put together by ordinary human beings working in concert with each other. When Glen and other "multidimensional visionaries" such as Stewart Swerdlow are asked about the New World Order conspiracy, they will frequently be com-

185

pelled to explain it by going back several millennia to a discussion of Atlantis. The basic story they tell is that the New World Order, the Illuminati, the Montauk Project, underground bases, and alien abductions are all very connected. These scenarios are outgrowths of an interplanetary war that took place in antediluvian times and which continue to play out covertly in our present.

The following is an excerpt of an interview I conducted with Glen Pruitt in which he discusses the underground Atlantean technology reclamation projects that he says employed Phil Schneider. He also describes the effects of the Orion Wars of the Atlantean era that are still being felt today. Glen reveals what he believes to be his father's role in the infamous contract between Naval Intelligence and Grey aliens and his mother's possible role in the financing of the Montauk Project.

Glen's insights are offered here as a possible larger perspective from which to view Phil Schneider's claims and the otherwise disjointed stories that run rampant on the Internet and in various fringe publications. Please do not accept them at face value. Use your own discernment. At times, it sounds like he is covering for his father when he claims the atrocities at Montauk occurred in a parallel reality. Hopefully, the interview will shed light on the bigger picture behind the death of Phil Schneider as well as other secret activities such as Montauk, Dulce, and Area 51.

Pruitt: The overriding consciousness of our Earth is in reconciling what happened to the Atlanteans... which is that they were wiped out by an alien race.

Bruce: By which alien race?

Pruitt: Actually, it was a group of alien races. A mixture of everything from Pleiadians and Greys to everything...

Bruce: And Draconians? Isn't that the confederacy that many people call the Orion Group?

Pruitt: Well, this was part of the Orion Wars. They were after control of the Akashic Record. The Akashic Record is a multidimensional computer complex which is made up of the gravitational fields of all of the planetary bodies in this system and the way all these planetary bodies in this system interact with all the planetary bodies of the systems that are in alternate universes. The Akashic Record is a ring that goes through the universes in a spiral formation. It's actually a double helix spiral. The fact is that this thing exists makes it easier to travel from universe to universe if you're going between the parallel universes in our solar system.

Bruce: Isn't the Orion consciousness the one behind the negative Montaukian groups?

Pruitt: In their universe, yes. In our universe, the majority of these alien groups are really regretful of what they did and have already evolved in consciousness.

Bruce: But that universe and that reality are impinging on this consciousness...

Pruitt: Exactly. The majority of your incidences like in *Fire In the Sky* are done more by aliens who are crossing over via the Montaukian portals. The average abduction scenario has been done by local Greys who have a treaty with the Federal Government – with the Navy anyway – to exchange technology for DNA and various reproductive materials. They hoped to revitalize their species and not go extinct which they were looking at doing within two generations.

Bruce: You've also said that Area 51, where Phil worked, is a base from which the Montauk Prime folks are operating in our universe.

Pruitt: Area 51 is actually several bases, only one of which is Montaukian. The underground base which extends from Sedona to Las Vegas is huge, yet only one of the bases at Area 51 is engaged in reverse engineering of alien technology.

There are also force fields still in operation around the major temples of the underground Atlantean city-state. This was an emergency evacuation site for the Atlanteans which they had to abandon for their own safety when the DNA retrovirus of the Orions started removing their higher faculties and psychic brain functions.

This, by the way, is why we have such problems with rhinoviruses such as colds and the flu today. They are degenerate forms of that plague which is, in fact, what REALLY wiped out Atlantis.

The continental destruction was caused by the incapacitated high priests who did not remember how to use their technology properly because they were afflicted by the virus from the wars. It was an accident caused by improper use of equipment designed to prevent earthquakes and do weather control, etc. After the accident, the elders of Atlantis realized that the same equipment was available to those underground, and when the virus began affecting those within, they activated an emergency plan which ejected all the people within the technology sectors and the temples and erected force fields around them.

This, of course, kept the Orions from getting what they really wanted. When they finally fought their way in, the fields kept them out.

Bruce: You've said that there are more Montauk Prime bases springing up all over the world lately: in China, New Zealand and Turkey to name a few.

Pruitt: In scanning the bases, I realize they are little more than listening posts and "weather stations" for etheric multidimensional energy. They are also installations for the siphoning off of energy and the dispersal of energy frequencies for purposes unknown. I feel it goes beyond simple mind control of the masses. I think they are attempting to avert what they consider to be a disaster of Biblical proportions. That of our waking up! That is, waking up our higher mental faculties which were lost to the viruses of the Orion wars. If we were able to regain those abilities, we could band together mentally and alter the vibrational prime note of the Sol system and cut them off and out of our universe. We would also be consciously aware of their chicanery and would probably begin operations to lock them into their own universes permanently.

Bruce: Is there now an Atlantean recovery mission beneath Montauk under the old submarine base?

Pruitt: If there is anything there, it's the Atlantean recovery project which, from a general citizenry perspective, could be just as scary.

Bruce: I heard stuff going on underground when I was there.

Pruitt: Yeah, but it's not Montaukian. It's an Atlantean Reclamation project which is more of an Illuminati thing than it is a New World Order thing. That's one of the things that I think we have to learn to distinguish. The New World Order originates in Montauk Prime while the Illuminati is of Earth in this timeline or reality. The NWO and Montauk originate in a parallel universe.

Bruce: Would the Illuminati be allied more with the Sirian/Semite consciousness?

Prime: Yes. This is why Hitler, being a puppet of the Montaukian New World Order, went after the Jews — because the Illuminati is Semite. What I'm getting also is that the Semites were a people that maintained their mental faculties. They were an Atlantean subspecies that maintained their faculties better than most other humans. This is why they were enslaved by the aliens who controlled Egypt. It is why the Semites were capable of magic.

Bruce: Am I correct in saying that the Sirians were the aliens controlling Egypt at that time?

Pruitt: I get that they were a Sirian-human blend. They had the elongated heads. Anyway, they were from this timeline and are associated with the Illuminati. I get that the Illuminati sells the Montaukian New World Order groups stuff and that the NWO sells the Illuminati stuff. Where they are not working at cross-purposes, they will do an uneasy truce to work together.

Bruce: The Illuminati is pro-Jewish and the Montauk group is Aryanist.

Pruitt: The Illuminati is really Mediterranean.

Bruce: I thought it was Masonic.

Pruitt: Different subspecies. Now, keep in mind that the Masons originally came from the Mediterranean but the Free and Accepted Masons of Scotland is a Johnny-come-lately Masonic order. There are other older Masonic orders.

Bruce: Yes, of course, the Franc Masons of France and many others.

Pruitt: Basically, the Scottish Masons are the descendants of the Knights Templar, but the Knights Templar are not associated with the original Masonic groups, the older ones of which are actually now very much in control of the Muslim world and Persia. The Masonic order in Old Europe and the Mediterranean is Illuminati. The Masonic order in America and the Scottish Rite is New World Order which has its origin in a parallel universe. That's the confusion. The group who's doing the Atlantean technology salvaging operations is a group of Illuminati-Masons. It's a Masonic group that has chosen a monastic life of secrecy. They consider what they're doing to be a sacred task.

Bruce: Archaeology and back-engineering?

Pruitt: Right, and they have assistance and aid from the military, and they pay for that assistance and aid by allowing them to have things that have been conserved already. Part of the aid and assistance by the military has been about slowly scanning every square inch of the planet with long wave radar capable of going down into the Earth some three or four hundred miles so they can find the deep cities. Actually, part of the way they've been doing that is by tracking where the tubes go. When they find four or five tubes going into a particular area, they know that they've got to check that area.

One of the things that protects the Atlantean cities to this day are dimensional-phase-shift-force-fields. That is, you can walk into the room and see nothing, yet the equipment is right there in front of you but vibrating a little differently than us so that we can't see it.

The Montaukians are ahead of us in creating wormhole travel systems, multidimensional computers, and communications. We are, however, ahead of them in electronics in general. Think of their systems as being tube-powered 1930's technology, yet they can teleport to other worlds and times with it. Very Philadelphia Experiment kind of stuff. They have some old Atlantean technology which they actually got from their Orion friends, yet ours is more advanced because we have had ours longer and had therefore more development time. It is my understanding that our government's first encounter with the Montaukians occurred with my father when he was commanding that minesweeper in Tokyo Harbor.

Bruce: So, it all started in Japan?

Pruitt: Remember, the Nazis were trying to help out their allies. In this case, the group that you know of that eventually went on to be in charge of the Montauk Project — they were originally Nazis who won the war on their world. So, the aliens who had helped them win the war over there gave them the technology to go to other Earths. They immediately started going to other Earths in the hopes of turning the tides in all the wars which is why we started to see a lot of UFOs cropping up in Nazi Germany at the end of the war. Vril craft and all this other stuff.

Bruce: Al Bielek says that the Philadelphia Experiment created a rip in space-time that allowed for an interdimensional invasion from another space/time continuum.

Pruitt: There had been earlier incursions but, yes, Project Rainbow blew the dimensional doors wide open. The Montaukians had already been here.

Let's put it this way. They were here from '41, '42 on. And they were still in force in the '50's and '60's. By "in force," I mean that they were here in battallion strength or perhaps even more. They withdrew their forces from the Antarctic only after Truman refused to back down after they buzzed the White House in the 1950's and even started releasing our own craft (Grey and Pleiadian technology) to go after them (with some success).

Bruce: Are they not here in force anymore?

Pruitt: Well, I'm being told "no" but not for anything that we did or for what the Japanese government did. More, it was that cities had to be closed due to earthquake damage. When you combine the fact that we started going after them in antigravity ships almost as good as theirs (which we got from the Greys) with better electronics...in fact, with the minor earthquake damage of the underground cities in the 1960's and early 1970's, they decided to pull out. They did not return in any significant force until the early 1980's — other than some spy missions and such that is.

Bruce: So, these Montaukian Nazis underground beneath Hiroshima — they had their first base in this reality under Japan?

Pruitt: No, they had their first base in this reality in the Antarctic. The second base was somewhere in Bavaria, and the third base was under Japan.

Bruce: Did they have a base at Montauk in this reality?

194

Pruitt: I'm being told, "no." They didn't have a base here; however, there are very natural portals at that location that with very low amounts of energy they can tap into. They have established a weather station there capable of controlling the weather and the ether of the wormholes. I'm getting that the real Montauk Project that they're in takes place both above and below ground and takes up half of Long Island.

Bruce: Half of Long Island?

Pruitt: Underground, anyway. It goes all the way to Brookhaven.

Bruce: Well, that's what Preston says is going on HERE, but you're saying that this facility is in a parallel universe. You are also saying that this presence of Montauk 5 and Montauk Prime beings was "in force" until the 1950's. They have since retracted due to earthquake damage and perhaps because they had other priorities. You also said that their presence increased again in the 1980's which leads us to now to the sticky present. I want to talk about what the presence of Montauk 5 and Montauk Prime is here today and the agenda to effect a New World Order shift here. What is the impact of all this Montaukian activity on mass consciousness in this reality?

Pruitt: Well, it's undecided at the moment. You've got a lot of dominant streams of consciousness fighting it out at the moment. You've got the alien propaganda machine and the section of the government that's using the alien propaganda machine to cover up Atlantean salvaging operations.

What an excellent disinformational ploy, to get all these conspiracy theorists focused on trying to get the government to own up to their connection to UFOs when, in fact, what they ought to be screaming about is that the U.S. Government is busting open all these Atlantean temples, robbing the technology, and allowing this technology to be released from government labs without any conservation of the originals or acknowledgment that we are a much older species.

There are, at present, five different groups within the military that have no sort of government oversight. You have the Naval Intelligence, Naval Ops group that was involved with the treaty with the Greys. That involved the technology swap for our genetic material and whatnot. That program has drawn to a close. We have another group within the government, and keep in mind that none of these groups really know about each other as they do the cell system of secrecy; however, they've run into each other and fights have broken out. There is another group of aliens that appear to be another strain of Greys. These other Greys have been working all over the Earth doing some sort of genetic experiment and manipulation for some two thousand years against everybody's will. That's part of a worldwide organization that involves all the major industrialized countries.

Bruce: In other words, these are international abductions, and they've been ongoing for two thousand years. This group is more negatively polarized than the other Greys with whom we signed the GREATA treaty in 1954.

Pruitt: Right. Those Greys were relatively benign. Part of that agreement was that no humans would be permanently injured.

Bruce: This would help explain some of the awful human mutilation stories coming out of Brazil, for example, the Chupa-Chupa phenomenon there of the 1970's when bodies would be found dangling from trees with every molecule of blood drained from their bodies.

Pruitt: Yeah, this group just had no ethical compunctions about how they obtained their genetic material. There are also humans involved in this Two Thousand Year Project that aren't subjects. They're allies. They're helping to cover up. They're cleaning up messes. They're getting paid.

Bruce: So, how does this Two Thousand Year Project relate to Montauk, if at all?

Pruitt: The universe that Montauk comes from — I'll call it Montauk Prime — the Montaukian humans are working hand-in-hand with the same race of Greys of the Two Thousand Year Project who are from our universe.

Bruce: Let me see if I understand this correctly. The Montaukian consciousness is Orion-based from another universe where the Orion conflict is still happening? Their consciousness is all about control, war, and domination.

Pruitt: (Drawing the multiversal map) OK, these are the parallel universes that I get are most intermixed with us. We've got several different Montauks. Here, we've got Montauk Prime. We're going to have to go back 70 million years to the Orion Wars which is where we got our moon. The Moon was the Battlestar that they came here in which blew up Maldek as they came through and created the asteroid belt. It then had to slow itself down by passing through the atmosphere of Mars, ripping away the atmosphere of Mars, and then getting caught in orbit by Earth. The Earth's orbit was destabilized at that time by a piece of Maldek causing the axial tilt. We even know where the asteroid hit. It hit in the Yucatan peninsula. The Orion Wars also occurred in Montauk Prime which is the universe where, in our era, the Nazis won the Second World War in conjunction with the Orion Group. Then, we have the parallel universe next to it which I'm going to call America Prime. This is where the Montauk Project is American. It's an officially-sanctioned project. Elements of this America Prime government work with our government here in the Atlantean recovery project. In fact, they met for the first time by leaving a message in a newly discovered temple just so they could be contacted.

Bruce: So, these guys are the "good" Montauk?

Pruitt: These are the guys that developed equipment that works out of the crown chakra that allows agents and materiel to go back and forth. They actually do it through a form of consciousness involving radionics, hypnosis, and electromagnetic fields to amplify the state of consciousness.

In some ways, the America Prime universe is like our idea; sort of like the America of the 1930's. They recovered from the Depression. There's nothing but promise and massive technological advances. They wipe out the Nazis very quickly. There's no lack of will in America. The Nazis invade France. They invade Belgium. Immediately, America responds. Period. "You invade the friends of our allies, you invade US!" And the Japanese, because they see how quickly we mobilized and started dumping tons of materiel on the Germans...the Japanese never even bombed Pearl Harbor. A very different world.

Here, look at this. This is the way the universes are arranged. We have Earth 9, a continuous Atlantean civilization that was never invaded. The one next to it is Earth 8. The Orions were pacified when they arrived on Earth so the humans and aliens work together. In this next universe, Earth 7, the Orions killed all the humans. The next one is us, Earth 6, with our Atlantean salvaging operations. Now, in this Atlantean continuous civilization universe over here, Earth 9, there was never an Orion war. They don't even have a moon. There are no monthly cycles in women. They only get pregnant when they want to. They aren't tied to gravity and the planet itself vibrates at a higher frequency.

Bruce: Montauk 3 is the one where we nuked ourselves. Was that the one where the bomb went over Los Alamos or the one where the bomb went over New York?

Pruitt: The one where the bomb went over New York is Montauk Prime. The nuclear holocaust at Los Alamos is Montauk 3.

Bruce: And Montauk 4 is the one where the humans have ascended and left. Montauk 5 is Nazis-in-hiding with an extensive underground base in Antarctica, the same guys who built the secret operational base on the Montauk of their world described in all the Montauk books. 6 is us. Montauk 7 is where the humans are all dead.

Pruitt: Yeah, but they died 70 million years ago during the Orion Wars. That's another world where there's no moon because the moon crashed into the Earth and that was it.

Bruce: Is a lot of Atlantean technology off-planetary technology?

Pruitt: No, no! A lot of alien technology is ATLANTEAN technology which was taken off-world. Everybody keeps thinking that all these aliens are more advanced than us. No! These aliens are living off of Atlantean scrap!

Bruce: So, what you're saying is that this Earth is the nexus.

Pruitt: I am saying that the three races of man (Neanderthal, Cro-Magnon, and homo sapiens) have been in existence in this solar system for over 300 million years. There are plenty of aliens out there that have their own technology, and there are aliens races that are older and have ascended. There are alien races that are older and that have better technology. But, all of the alien races that are here today are here because of the Atlantean connection and because they are seeking to siphon off the mental psychic energy that is being generated as we ascend because they're hoping to use the energy as a catalyst to help them ascend without having to go through the trouble of evolving.

Bruce: Let's talk a little bit about the interplay of these parallels. You were saying that our solar system is uniquely located within the toroidal flow; that makes it a portal to all the parallels. This is why there are so many ET and other dimensional races here now, on our world, observing us.

Pruitt: Another reason is because this is the easiest place to get between the universes. So, we're in the highway. A lot of them aren't even staying here. We just catch glimpses of them as they pass through.

Bruce: It seems that these parallel universes are each expressing their own prevailing mass consciousnesses.

Pruitt: The parallel universes' consciousnesses affect each other, particularly at specific times of the year. There are astrological configurations. When you start aligning gravity wells, you start getting a massive crossover of consciousness.

Bruce: Preston and Al have said that your dad issued their paychecks; that he was their boss. Are you saying that this was in another universe; that Preston and Al have got their universes mixed up like Phil Schneider did?

Pruitt: Right, but what I'm also getting from the Al and Preston scenario – and Duncan, for that matter — is that it's not just that they got their universes mixed up. There is an easier way to describe this. Where the Nazis lost the war and operate out of the Antarctic (which is right next to our universe) in Montauk 5, they're limited in resources and they're having to operate without world government knowledge. They are the ones who have the underground base in Montauk on their world. They're not only trying to do the New World Order in their universe, they're trying to do it in ours. They're the ones that are doing the sex slave (Monarch) programming.

Bruce: Basically, you're saying that after Al and Duncan jumped off the *U.S.S. Eldridge* during the Philadelphia Experiment, in our universe, they landed in the parallel universe that we're calling Montauk 5 and were then sent back to our own space-time continuum? The Jack Pruitt that they are talking about is the version from Montauk 5...

Pruitt: Who was a Nazi sympathizer who was handling the Nazi gold that the Nazis managed to get over to America, undercover, to convert it into currency in order to buy the equipment that they needed to buy.

Bruce: So that did not happen in our timeline.

Pruitt: Right. I finally got the whole thing straightened out with my dad. My father worked for a mortgage company that was owned by Republic National Bank. My mother was the CEO's personal assistant. Before then, she was in charge of approving all loans. In actuality, if there were any Montaukian financial transactions in this universe, they would probably have been handled by my mother. I'm finding out all this weird crap about my mother. She was married five times — had children by each marriage here in New York. I didn't find out about that until she was dead. There was a lot of weird stuff about my mother that's only recently been coming out.

Bruce: So, what do you suppose that the Montauk 5 version of your father did or was doing in this reality? What was the purpose of his coming here?

Pruitt: In view of all of the electronics companies in Dallas, he could have been going to buy things for the project in Montauk Prime. Remember, we're the older and more developed universe in the stream. We are the Atlantean salvagers. I really get that our technology here is much higher than Montauk Prime's. Their Montauk Project involved a lot of vacuum tubes! That's one of the things that Preston was talking about...that the field generators that they were using all used tubes. That's all 1930's era for us!

Bruce: In what capacity did your father sign the GREATA treaty; with what authority? Who gave him the right to represent us or our government?

Pruitt: I think he was just a witness.

Bruce: He was not the executor –

Pruitt:— and a translator. He was not the signator.

Bruce: Who would that be? Truman?

Pruitt: Yeah.

Bruce: So, how was your dad able to translate for the Greys?

Pruitt: What I was just being told is that it was high magick. I've got a real tradition of high magick in my family. People forget that the military trains its officers. You know, everybody keeps asking me, did my father know this? Did my father know that? The scary part is that I get it was my mother that was Montaukian. I can remember my mother doing some hateful things to people that had screwed her over, and she was very big in the Republican party. Henry Kissinger came over to have dinner with —not my father — my mother! Haig came over to NMI (New Mexico Military Institute, a military boarding school) when I was there because I was her son. I remember Mom telling me, "By the way, I've asked Secretary Haig if he would mind speaking at NMI. Would you mind going out to dinner with him?"

"OK, Mom."

The next thing I know, I'm being called up to the school Commandant's office and him saying, "Mr. Pruitt. Here's your pass. I understand you're going to be having dinner with Secretary Haig this evening."

"Yes Sir!"

Bruce: Tell me what your mother's role in the Montauk Project has been. Was she a financial officer?

Pruitt: What's strange is that she went from being one of the Chief Loan Officers to being the personal private assistant to the CEO of Republic National Bank.

Bruce: That sounds like a step down to me: going from having the power to make big loans to being like the CEO's secretary.

Pruitt: Then, she quit when she got married.

Bruce: That wasn't unusual in those days...

Pruitt: What I'm suggesting is: what if that's one of the liaisons? What if she flipped over to the CEO because it enabled her to have full access to everything that went across the CEO's desk? Remember, this is a woman who could walk into the CEO's office and say, "Sign here, sign here, sign here, thank you."....."Uh, what did I sign?".....

"Routine paperwork." Men like that have to sign so much paperwork that they have to trust their assistant to not be screwing them over and running the company into the ground. And who can they trust more than the former Chief Loan Officer? What I get is that she was responsible for transferring gold. Then, she proceeded to completely change. I have to wonder if she was a "walk-in." That's the feeling that I get.

Bruce: What kind of walk-in? What's the agenda of the walk-in?

Pruitt: I'm getting that they just yanked her and substituted, and it was the substitution that was Ruth Bowen ever since.

Bruce: Was this the Montauk Prime version of your mom? Do you think that your father was aware of this about her?

Pruitt: Maybe on the other side; when the programming kicked in. It's going to be very interesting to find out how much of this my father is aware of.

Bruce: Are you going to tell him all of this?

Pruitt: Not over the phone.

Bruce: This is very strange. Where are all these children? Do you know?

Pruitt: Yes.

Bruce: Are they here in New York City?

Pruitt: Yes. That's part of why I was drawn back to Queens, where I was born.

Bruce: You said that your father is willing to come forward and actually talk about the UFO sinking his boat during the '50's in Japan – your father will come forward with that story?

Pruitt: Well, he's told me that if I really wanted to, I could find evidence under the Freedom of Information Act of what happened to his minesweeper. It's still definitely not OK to talk about the GREATA treaty. I get that he doesn't have any oaths about Montauk, but I think that part of the preprogramming, during most of my life with him, shielded him from knowing what was going on. It has only been in the last five years that part of that anti-remembrance programming has started breaking down. His wife, Barbara, has told me that sometimes he wakes up yelling and he never used to do that.

Bruce: You said he made an interesting comment to you over the phone last night about how you should start thinking about flying down to Dallas for his funeral.

Pruitt: Yeah, he told me that if I was really serious about wanting to pursue this; then, maybe it was time for him to die.

Bruce: Really? So, this statement was made in the

context of your looking into these issues and asking the questions that we're asking right now?

Pruitt: Yeah. Well, it was in the context of him handing over the proof.

Bruce: Everyone would sure love to see "the proof!" But you're looking at me like you can't talk about it! It would appear that your family is deeply embedded in inter-parallel universe activities. You mentioned before that the Montauk 5 universe was concerned with trying to implement the New World Order in our reality.

Pruitt: Because, right now, their consciousness level is too low to be able to take over Montauk 5. Their goal is to be able to shift the consciousness of our reality which is Prime 6, the Atlantean salvaging civilization; because if they can create their New World Order and actually take over the consciousness of our world, that will give them the energy they need to significantly affect the consciousness of their universe. What we have on our side, however, is help from America Prime.

Not only do you have the government effectively doing the work of the New World Order by opening up all these Atlantean temples and using all the technology that they find there, you have civilian groups opening up temples in secret. They're salvaging stuff and using it to put over-writing frequencies into our grid. But, what we have more of than just about anywhere else is angelic involvement because we are the closest to making a non-technological leap.

Bruce: A consciousness leap.

Pruitt: Which is the most powerful kind of leap possible. That's one of the reasons we're so susceptible to Montauk 5; because all they have to do is suddenly twist the ambient energy in their direction. Just skew it a little bit, and what they end up with is us not ascending but entering a state of consciousness that is more easily unified and directed. It's kind of like the line between love and hate. The line between ascension and mass mind control is very fine because when you're ascending, you're mind controlling yourself. You're changing your belief structure at the subatomic level.

Bruce: Would you say that there are factions on Earth that don't want this information to come out or is it really the factions from the other universes that don't want this information available to people in our reality — because you were saying that Phil Schneider got killed by a faction in our reality?

Pruitt: A faction in our reality that didn't want the Atlantean salvaging operations to come to light. I do believe that in Montauk 5 they may be getting ready to do a takeover coup of several of their world's largest governments. One of the reasons they've collapsed the Russians everywhere they can, including in our universe, is because the Russians were most resistant to Nazi mind control because they're already so paranoid.

Bruce: Well, the Russians had their own brand of

mind control, too. They were developing psychotronic weapons –

Pruitt: Right, but theirs were for a different purpose. They were to maintain an ideological perspective rather than to keep people from remembering things.

Bruce: Basically, what you're saying is that the agenda of Montauk 5 is to take over this reality.

Pruitt: Well, their intention was to sway our consciousness enough to enable them to take over theirs a bit easier. Anyway, I get that in this reality, the whole concept of a New World Order is basically falling apart. They did not succeed in what they were attempting to do which was to get us to rewrite our Constitution. They wanted to create a situation where we could merge with the EC and then start gobbling up all the other countries on Earth. That aspect of reality, I get, has been shifted. Phil Schneider's life itself, and his death, was done to shift consciousness.

Bruce: When I asked you last year how many people had been sent through Montaukian time tunnels, you said 250. When I asked you again a couple weeks ago, you said thousands had been sent into the future, never to return. I called you on it and you responded that it all must have happened within the last year.

So, the folks in Montauk Prime would like to take over our world. One way is by sending all these people into the future to try to make all of the parallel futures the way that they want it to be and this has been happening a lot in recent months.

Pruitt: Right. Massive operations within the last year. And in the past two months, thousands more.

Bruce: Is this all in Montauk Prime?

Pruitt: This is in all the Montauk worlds. They are attempting to bring all of the futures into alignment with what they want with the belief that America Prime, us, and all of the stalwarts that have managed to fend them off will just be blipped out of existence. They think it's just a matter of putting in enough power to create a massive enough change. You're dealing with a kind of a communistic hive mind that is incapable of seeing that it's not working; that's unable to determine the causes for why it's not working. It's a bureaucracy that thinks that since it has decreed that it is so, then it will be so. They just have to figure out how to make it work. They haven't caught on that it just is not possible; the multiverse is constructed in such a way as to preclude anybody doing what they're trying to do.

Bruce: So, the Montaukians keep trying to go into the future to change the present. You've said that you can only change the past or future by changing the present. Reality travels out in ripples; into the past and future from the present.

Pruitt: Right. They key is distinguishing between what is truly yours and what they're attempting to impose.

211

Bruce: They're attempting their invasion through the human soul.

Pruitt: Because they can only get to us by having us making choices. By feeding us misleading information, by confusing our little consciousness, and our capability to mentate, they win. For us, the key is how do we get to the point to where we know what is truly ours and no one else's? That is what we're here to do. Ultimately, for every evil act, there's something good that comes out of it. That's what they're doing for us. They are forcing humanity to wake up.

Bruce: So, that's why they can't win. It's a yin-yang tailspin!

Pruitt: Well, they can't win unless we give up. They have no jurisdiction where humans have learned to control their vibration. In other words, they can't control humans who are completely responsible for their consciousness.

Bruce: So, what would you recommend for dealing with this Montaukian interdimensional attack?

Pruitt: Well, first, you have to cut yourself from your lateral connections to your parallel selves. Vertical connections to your higher aspects are OK. Lateral connections don't really serve you. Lateral connections are real-time. Your alternates are in the same time stream as you. They're needing to make different decisions than you are. As a matter of fact, that's how consciousness affects itself from universe to universe. If we ascend...if our vibration goes up that high...then our vibration will adjust to them. It'll raise their vibration until they cut it. Otherwise, it's going to totally destabilize them.

Bruce: So, that's why there are mind control projects in this reality: to keep consciousness within a certain bandwidth.

Pruitt: Basically, we deal with it by cutting ourselves off from the lateral connections; by raising our vibration consciously, through active will and by remembering to do constant self-checking: "Is this mine? Is this programmed? Is this bleedthrough?" If we reject their reality and stick with our truth — a truth that is in harmony with ascension, in harmony with Atlantis or the idea of a long stable existence — then that's what we'll get.

Bruce: So, you were saying that, 70 million years ago, the Orion retrovirus removed our higher psychic brain functions. The destruction of Maldek and subsequent axial tilt of the Earth has blown out our thymus chakra and kept the planet off-kilter and us from receiving the cosmic energies for proper consciousness and food nourishment across the board. How could we ever hope to recover our lost faculties while everything is in such disarray?

Pruitt: Software patches. Rewriting the way we think.

Bruce: How does this work?

Pruitt: Slowly but surely. What's happening is that we're learning to reconnect our thymuses without the higher brain functions. What's going to end up happening is that the thymus is going to download enough energy to jumpstart our brains.

Bruce: You said something interesting before: that each planet in the solar system is representative of each chakra in our body. As the thymus represents Maldek, which was shattered, our thymus chakra is shattered.

Pruitt: Which means Earth is actually the seat of our ego. Mars is our heart. Maldek was the thymus or high heart. Ego is third, the solar plexus. Mercury is first, the root chakra. Venus is the second, the creative/sexual chakra.

Bruce: You've said that this whole media blitz about the UFO phenomenon is really a cover for the Atlantean salvaging operations; yet, I get that there's a lot of UFO activity.

Pruitt: Oh, that's not to say that there isn't all kinds of UFO activity happening, but the government is using the UFO movement as a disinformation campaign. As long as they keep denying that there are any UFOs, nobody is looking at what they're really doing.

We are a planet that is shifting in vibration. The Luciferian regime is attempting to slow down that shift as much as they can and skew it off in their direction. The "good guys" are attempting to speed it up in another direction. Right now, the

Luciferians are ahead because they've succeeded in controlling the schools for a long time through subtle manipulations. It all started in earnest after the roaring '20's in the early '30's. 1932 was the institution of the Federal Reserve.

People don't realize that the Depression didn't need to happen. Nothing was lost during the Depression. Companies were still companies. They still owned everything they owned and employed people. What was lost was the so-called value of their stock. This didn't change the fact that the company was still worth something. The reason for the Depression was perception. Everyone who had cash started hoarding it. Because we were on the gold standard at the time, they couldn't just print money. The ratio of paper to gold was determined by Congress. That was what determined the value of currency. There was a limited amount of currency out there. So, when they had the runs on the banks because everybody wanted their money back because they were afraid of what was happening, all of the paper money got dumped into the economy. There wasn't any more money left for growth, and we had a depression. But, it was all about perception. If they'd left the money in the bank, there still would have been enough money to run the country.

The Federal Reserve was created specifically so that they could take control of the currency out of the hands of Congress to better enable them to manipulate the population.

Bruce: Who's "they"?

Pruitt: In this case, we're talking about the five families.

Bruce: What are the "five families" all about?

Pruitt: I would say that they are part of long term genetic experimentation. We're talking about the Queen Mother. We're talking about the Kaiser's family, the Emperor of China's family, Japan's family, and the Rockefellers. We're talking about some very specific families of money, and I think that they were genetically engineered so that it would be very easy to put ideas into their heads.

Bruce: Who genetically-engineered them? Aliens?

Pruitt: No. Nazis.

Bruce: And the Nazis are carrying out a multidimensional Luciferian agenda.

Pruitt: Yes.

Bruce: This sounds a lot like what David Icke says: that the Nazis, the Five Families, and the multinational banking and petroleum cartels are part of a New World Order conspiracy that has it's origin in a Luciferian consciousness in the 4th Dimension. I guess he says it's coming from Fourth Density only because that's the next step up in vibration.

Pruitt: But it isn't what's next. What's next is the integration of 3D reality and time so that we can then manipulate time and be in the 5th Dimension.

All the 4th Dimension is is time. The 5th Dimension is when we can control time. We will have gone beyond the concept of time.

This is the deal with multidimensional reality and why we would be better off doing away with the concept of Karma. Karma is a Luciferian construct which keeps us from being in the PRESENT moment. Karma can't exist in our life if our consciousness is truly and fully in the present moment. Since all that exists is the primordial *Om*, from a macroscopic perspective of reality, you must throw away the whole concept of past lives or bother yourself with the idea of your "parallel lives".

Every memory that we have exists in its own vibratory algorithm or dimension. Therefore, there can't be a true connection as in "our soul was there and now it's here." Whatever our consciousness is generating, in terms of our energy and vibratory algorithm, is in the present moment. Karma, which is basically holding a stuck and blocked thought-form in your consciousness that you totally screwed-up, totally shifts your vibratory algorithm. That's what the whole bit about "letting go of judgement" is really about.

18

THE REPTOIDS

Among Phil Schneider's most outlandish claims were his repeated references to his involvement in the "Dulce Wars." He may even have been the originator of this legend which has been passed down in the intervening years by fringe conspiracy writers. This deadly clash between 60 government employees and several "tall, big-nosed Greys" supposedly took place in the Dulce, New Mexico underground base in 1979.

It is too easy to dismiss these remarkable claims, but to avoid them would be to miss a crucial element of Phil's message and of his untimely death. Plus, there would not be too much else to write about after ascertaining that a series of local law enforcement personnel had suspiciously botched their jobs. Phil's claims are what got him on the lecture circuit to begin with and are likely related to what got him killed. I am also deeply aware that to take some of Phil's claims seriously could have the effect of transferring a certain lack of credibility to me.

At the time that Phil Schneider lectured about the secret reptilian invasion of the Government, the Internet was not nearly as widespread as it has since become and Phil's eerie testimony did not travel very far. Since his murder, however, the simultaneous advent of both the Internet and the conspiracy author David Icke has done much to give a context to Phil's references and to popularize his warnings about a reptilian invasion of Earth. Indeed, with Icke's help — and just in time for the Chinese astrological Year of the Dragon, no less — the reptilian aliens have successfully completed their invasion of conspiracy literature and seized the public's imagination.

In the realm of conspiracy, nothing since the airing of the *Alien Autopsy* footage has stirred up the amount of contention as the phenomenon of David Icke with the release of his book *The Biggest Secret* and the launching of his inflammatory website in April of 1999.

With a shrillness that is unmatched, David Icke claims that the world's most prominent geopolitical players and the governments and multinational industries that they operate are all fronts for interdimensional reptilian puppet masters. With all of this, Phil Schneider would have heartily agreed.

The controlling reptilians Icke describes are semiphysical inhabitants of "fourth density," a plane of reality that is at a higher vibratory rate than the material 3D world. The reptilians' domination-oriented consciousness is said to resonate and express itself in the physical realm of our third density reality. How? Via the institutions, the ideologies, and the DNA of the reptilian hybrid custodial caste that comprises the world's royal and elite bloodlines. To document his case, Icke has meticulously and convincingly traced the steps of these elites and their establishments over the millennia.

Despite the audacity and the weirdness of Icke's claims, the sheer mass of historical data he has accumulated to substantiate them is impressive. Whatever credibility this feat has earned him, however, is completely ruined by his ongoing fervent and surrealistic denunciations of public figures. An example would be his claim that Queen Elizabeth and the Queen Mother are, in reality, "shapeshifting reptoids" intent on the satanic ritualistic eating of babies and the drinking of freshly-sacrificed human blood.

While it is amusing to picture these comically lurid tableaux, and it is quite FUN to pretend for a moment that such stories are "true" (two thumbs up for entertainment value!), he has baited himself for derision with these ridiculously wild and defamatory remarks. Icke's sensationalistic slant has discredited the genuine value of some of his information. It is a disservice to the serious scholarship that has been done on the subject matter by others and by himself.

His most cherished refrain, "shapeshifting reptilian," is also his most misleading. All human beings share some DNA structures with reptilians. In fact, all biological Earthlings share a lot of the same genetic codes. It is said that we humans share up to 80% of our genetics with SPIDERS! Furthermore, human beings possess a "reptilian brain" located at the very core of our noodle. Indeed, the "intelligent" gray matter of the outer neocortex appears to be abruptly grafted on top of this reptilian core.

Icke has had an excellent article posted on his website about the characteristics of this inner reptilian brain and the functions and attributes of the reptilian level of consciousness that exists within all humans. It is not surprising to learn that these human reptilian brain characteristics of territoriality, domination, and addiction are what typify the qualities of our supposed fourth density reptoid overlords, something Icke duly points out.

The existence of the reptilian brain and the limbic system within every human being are the first clue that the reptoid phenomenon is more complex and multifaceted than Icke's overly-literal shapeshifting accusations would indicate. Dragons appear extensively in worldwide mythology. If only one could ask England's patron saint, George, who was so enshrined for slaying dragons: "Exactly what animal were you killing?"

Was the dragon symbolic, literal, or both? Besides our shared DNA codes with reptilians and our reptilian brain stem, there is also an archetypal reptilian resonance which echoes from the mists of time and legend, perhaps the legacy of the dinosaurs. This does not make any person a "shapeshifting reptilian" per se. A human being may have a resonance with reptilian energy or even direct resonance with evil extraterrestrial fourth density reptilians. A psychic adept may be able to perceive such reptilian energetics overlaying the field of a human being or to perceive other-dimensional reptilian aspects of that person's soul; but, that is still NOT the same thing as a HUMAN person BEING a "shapeshifting reptilian"!

While there are numerous strange accounts of the fourth density reptoids' ability to project holograms that make them appear as physical humans for limited amounts of time, it is highly doubtful that this is what is occurring with the Queen Mother. Even by most far-out eyewitness testimonies, no reptoid could sustain the ruse of appearing human for twenty-four hours a day, seven days a week. If the Queen Mother is part reptoid, and it is unlikely that there is reliable evidence of that, it is far more likely that she could be a host for a nonphysical reptilian entity.

Icke's miscommunication comes from his overly literal 3D read of fourth density phenomena. This is done either out of a genuine (if misguided) sense of urgency on his part, or it is simply a conspiracy huckster's catchy sales pitch. Could his tack render him the next *Chicken Little* or

The Boy Who Cried Wolf? To be fair, Icke's avocation is not easy. Fourth density phenomena do easily translate into third density language and proving their "truth" is a challenge at best. In addition to many other terms, fourth density has been variously described in our language as the astral plane, dream-time, or the imaginal realm. Fourth density is an order of reality that interacts with the physical plane. There is an archetypal or mythical quality to it as opposed to the familiar "hardness" of 3D reality. Even so, this does not minimize the "reality" of fourth density or its denizens at all. Dreams, ideas, and beliefs literally shape and inform the material world. Without them, no wars would be fought, and nothing would be bought, etc. Theoretical physicists are currently working out the long division that would mathematically explicate the hyperdimensions that interpenetrate the physical world. However, the more right-brained members of our species and countless native cultures have forever recognized these other realms.

In any case, Icke is by no means an innovator in the field of reptiliana. My own first encounter with "reptoids" was in 1991 in a far-out channeled newsletter called the *Revelations of Awareness.* The vivid descriptions of planetoids hauling millions of invading reptoids Earthward at the speed of gravity "18 times faster than the speed of light" was put forth as gripping drama. This same mythos made worldwide headlines in 1997 with the advent of the Hale-Bopp comet and the liturgy that resulted in the mass suicide of the Heaven's Gate cult.

There has always been a basic incongruity within the reptoid mythos as promoted by Phil Schneider, David Icke, and others which short circuits logic. Why are there flotillas of space rocks bearing giant man-eating lizards "coming to get us" when it is also purported that the

"Lizzies" were always here and genetically-engineered the human race from day one? It has also been said that the reptilians have been constantly tweaking human history towards their nefarious ends using their evil time travel tricks. How are they supposed to have full mastery of our time, reality, and genetics when they are schlepping their way over toward us, en masse, still yet to "arrive"? Maybe, as author Stewart Swerdlow (*Montauk: The Alien Connection*) suggests, it is a matter of human beings awakening to their presence that has made them appear, in an archetypal sense, to be "arriving" to the growing body of those who perceive them?

The *Cosmic Awareness*, as channeled by Paul Shockley, was the early-nineties forerunner to David Icke's website as a reptoid information clearinghouse. This publication indicated that many of the political leaders of our world had been "switched" with cloned "robotoids" that were piloted by interdimensional reptilians, etc. Spurred on by the reptoid specter raised by *Cosmic Awareness*, I bought two books by the self-described ex-government cryptographer and Sumerian scholar, R.A. Boulay, *Flying Serpents and Dragons* and *Dragon Power* (published in 1990 and 1992, respectively). Boulay adds his own insights to Zachariah Sitchen's (author of *The Twelfth Planet*) information and basically says that the Annunaki were a custodial crossbreed of reptoid/primate/hominids. The Annunaki were a "royal" half-caste engineered to lord over the slave caste created to mine gold for the aliens and to do other menial tasks.

Boulay's story dovetailed quite nicely with the Merovingian myth about the origins of their bloodline as outlined in the cult classic *Holy Blood, Holy Grail* by Baigent, Lincoln and Leigh. The ancient Merovingian legend goes that the queen was already pregnant by the king and went for a swim in the ocean whereupon she was raped by a "Quinotaur." The resulting hybrid offspring, Merovee, became the founder of the Merovingian blood-line into which all the royal houses of Europe have since striven to marry. This has all been detailed ad nauseam in numerous subsequent books by Baigent-Lincoln-Leigh and by Laurence Gardner in his *Bloodline of the Holy Grail*. The present generations of their offspring are the self-same folks implicated by Icke & Co. to be the fear-some reptoid half-breeds that are selling the rest of hu-manity out to the "microchipped" New World Order.

The Quinotaur figure is reminiscent of the Oannes character of Sumerian lore who would emerge from the sea and teach agriculture, literacy, and architecture to the primitive locals. This amphibian figure is also similar to the West African Dogon tribe's tales of "fishmen" from the stars who taught them math and astronomy. There is also the European children's fairy tale of the Frog Prince as well as the abiding obsession with dragons of the Chinese. "Japanese legends of serpent/dragon and human marriages, seductions, and liaisons abound," says Wm. Michael Mott in another excellent and extensively re-searched article recently posted on David Icke's website.

Many legends of the origins of certain Scottish clan names contain a similar story. For example, the name MacLaclan (MacLaughlin, McLoughlin, etc.) is said to derive from "Lakeland," the underwater kingdom (a la Atlantis). The daughter of the king of Lakeland, who was described as a large "dark" nonhuman sea creature, was said to have married an ancient warlord and thus founded the new dynasty. The name MacVeigh, along with its cognates such as MacFie, MacPhee and Duffy also have this legend. This underwater princess bride would seem to bear a not insignificant resemblance to "Nessie" the

Loch Ness Monster! These are the clans' own legendary accounts and not merely a smear by David Icke.

Given my interest with all of these related subjects, I was not surprised to discover that, according to Icke, I myself come from a big time "shapeshifting reptilian" bloodline. Furthermore, there are numerous references to my celebrated clan mate, Robert the Bruce, as being the founder of modern Freemasonry. The Masons are the subject of endless calumny and are implicated in nonstop satanic wrongdoing by Icke and other conspiratologists.

The upshot of my investigation into all of this human/reptilian weirdness is that I have trained myself not to believe or to judge anything anymore. I do my best to absorb data while endeavoring to discern its ideology and its agenda. This bizarre information is worthwhile to the degree it aids 3D-bound consciousness to understand multidimensionality. My assessment of the reptilian witch hunt is that it's just more of the same divisive disinformational nonsense that the reptilians and their half-caste "toadies" are accused of perpetrating on the rest of humanity. In any case, if Icke's website and literature can increase an awareness of and warn his audience about the evil reptoid within us all, I think the work he is doing is invaluable. If nothing else, it is excellent entertainment!

My quest to understand the full implications of Phil Schneider's death has thus taken us to the extreme end of the lunatic fringe so pervasive in our repressed culture. If, as Al Bielek has said on many an occasion, the Philadelphia Experiment gated in aliens en masse to our domain, we are only left with scraps of information upon which to base our conclusions. All we know for sure is that the truth is suppressed and that there are powerful forces in the military and Government keeping it that way. Nevertheless, truth continues to leak out.

19

REALITY CHECK

This book, which began as an investigation of Phil Schneider's death, actually became a probe of reality itself. When I first embarked on the research of Phil's story, I did not guess that a discourse would evolve about mind control, quantum realities and an alternate Philadelphia Experiment. Throughout this book, I have had no intention of proving anything other than that the circumstances surrounding Phil's death and its legal investigation are highly suspicious and in need of judicial review.

While convoluted parallel universe accounts can do little to vindicate Phil Schneider's death, they certainly are in the spirit of what he passionately lectured about during the last two years of his life. I have no doubt they are related to his urgent final message for the world.

Odd as it may sound, I have found the study of fringe conspiracy legends to be very worthwhile. Any story is ultimately irrelevant and useless to me outside of what it can teach me about Creation and the empowerment of humans via insights about how reality works. To this end, the scrutiny of Phil Schneider's tales of joint military-alien underground bases, the Philadelphia Experiment, and the Montauk Project has been quite useful. The chief benefit from the study of these nuclear-age pop cult legends is this: Everything you can imagine is true; so choose your thoughts thoughtfully. Choose your beliefs carefully and choose your REALITY wisely.

These legends contain wisdom about how reality works: from the spiritual, to the geopolitical, to the subatomic. It is cosmically humorous that these "crackpot" stories, so full of seemingly deranged allegations, actually do contain many practical and penetrating truths about consciousness and the nature of reality.

Having explored the hall of mirrors that is the realm of alien abductions, secret government time travel, and the more legitimate domain of quantum physics for some twenty years, I have arrived at another powerful understanding: the story itself, whether "true" or not, is beside the point. The story's *ideology* and *agenda* are what is of paramount importance. What does the story stand for? What does it ultimately generate and create? Who does the story serve and whom does it empower?

People get tripped up by thinking they need to commit to believing or disbelieving all these wild conspiracy tales when it is the whole construct of belief itself that needs to be examined more closely. This is especially relevant as belief is the most highly-trafficked commodity in human activity and impels virtually everything we do.

During the course of my investigative journeys, the "thought police" syndrome ran rampant among my peers as well as within myself. People feared for my sanity. My beliefs were constantly called into question. There was something distinctly medieval about the whole experience, like being purged in an "Anti Fada."

I had momentarily suspended my relatively conventional cluster of beliefs to explore unacceptable "lunatic fringe" beliefs and I literally lost friends as a result. I was excommunicated by those who could not handle it. I learned the hard way how even the suspicion of having beliefs that are grossly out of step with the general consensus can imbue one with the status of a pariah. This constant unspoken threat of disenfranchisement has people towing the line rather than thinking for themselves.

The "icky" and spooky conspiracy realm spoken of by Phil Schneider and a host of others is an assault on conventional sanity and is utterly repugnant to mentalities that are invested in conforming to the hegemony. This unfavorable reception is in part a reaction to some of the personalities who promote this subject matter. Some conspiracy proponents clearly have emotional issues that detract from their ability to communicate powerfully.

On the other hand, those who feel a need to bash Phil Schneider and the reality he described are overlooking valuable information as well as proclaiming their dogged allegiance to old guard mind patterns and core beliefs. This attitude is not much different from those who believe anything they read. I maintain that research into the eerie and the arcane is good cognitive gymnastics. Exercising your noodle in tandem with your intuitive and discerning faculties is not bad!

To call these conspiracy realm stories modern-day folklore could be a way to create a common ground between the skeptics who will hear none of this and the "true believers" who have a seemingly insatiable desire to believe anything weird. Folklore pertains to what some refer to as the imaginal realm. Determinists and materialists consider anything imaginary to be immaterial and therefore essentially nonexistent. They acknowledge the existence of archetypes but refuse to delve any deeper into their very function as the informing principles of the material world. On the other end of the mind-set spectrum, some hard-core New Agers call this same domain "fourth density" and will believe any old thing "channeled" by the Ashtar Command or the Pleiadians. This group appears to be in denial of their faculties of logic.

The term folklore will do nothing for Cynthia Drayer, Phil Schneider's ex-wife and the mother of his child. She maintains that Phil was lecturing from direct experience about the alien invasion of our world governments, that he was murdered for talking about it, and that his murder was covered up. It is our hope, as well as that of the rest of Phil's friends, that his case will one day be reopened so that justice may be obtained for his death.

EPILOGUE

You have now come to the end of one more chapter in the quest to uncover the truth concerning the Philadelphia Experiment and Montauk Project. Although there is still an effort to "murder" the story, more and more people are facing the fact that something important happened, and we are not being told the total truth.

As this very book was being edited by myself, I received a certified letter from an elderly lady who had studied the Philadelphia Experiment for well over twenty years. She had some information that she had never trusted with another researcher and felt that I should have it. It included two books that are now out of print: *After the Philadelphia Experiment* by Gray Barker and *The Jessup Dimension* by Anna Lykins Genzlinger. Unfortunately, when the lady sent me the information, she was feeling bad that day and failed to take the extra time and bother to certify the package. This was in spite of the fact that these were her only copies. The package never arrived!

In the course of ordinary business, most mail seems to come and go routinely. I do not have time to worry about conspiracy, however, if something is very important, I always sent it certified. For this package not to arrive would seem to show a concerted effort on someone's part to "murder" the story once again.

After a couple of months went by, I spoke to this lady and asked her if she could remember the most critical information that was in the package she sent. Her reply was more than a little interesting. First and foremost, she said that the information included a list of those who were aboard the *Eldridge* during the Philadelphia Experiment. The addresses and other information were old, but some of the people were still traceable.

There was also another story of a female researcher who had scoured the country looking for Mrs. Jessup and her husband. The theory here is that it was not the actual body of Morris K. Jessup that was found in the car in Florida so many years ago. Jessup's wife refused to identify the body. Ironically, the female researcher was subsequently visited by a "Mr. Wilson" from the Navy.

Another "Mr. Wilson" appeared when the aforementioned elderly lady wrote a letter to *Fate* magazine asking about Carlos Allende. Mr. Wilson incorrectly informed her that Allende had gone back to his home in Mexico. Of course, Allende was not from Mexico, and he was dead at the time of Mr. Wilson's response.

The most interesting story the elderly lady had to tell me was what Allende himself had said about the day of the Philadelphia Experiment. He was below decks aboard a merchant marine vessel, assumably the *USS Andrew Faruseth*, when he felt a sudden and significant thump to the ship and then heard a thunderous crash. Coming above decks, he saw that a UFO had crashed into another vessel, not the *Eldridge*, that was in the Philadelphia Naval Yard that day. This vessel was there to observe the experiment and housed Albert Einstein. One account says Einstein was there to try and stop the experiment. Those in charge were afraid the ship would sink and got Einstein off for his own safety. Once Einstein was aboard the *Faruseth* (assuming this was the ship), Allende was charged with soothing the old scientist and keeping him happy while he recovered from the shock of the incident. Allende took him to the galley for coffee, got him some blankets, a cabin to rest in and proceeded to pepper him with questions about UFO propulsion drives. Allende was fascinated with flying saucers and how they work but was not educated enough to ask all the right questions. After all, a saucer had been right in front of them and he wanted to know how in the world these flying saucers got from here to there. He pinned Einstein down and got him talking. Saying it was not that simple, Einstein sat there and told him everything he thought Allende could understand.

Allende also observed the deck of the *Eldridge* on that day and could not understand why people and the ship itself disappeared. At some point, he witnessed an energy field up close but it is not clear if it emanated from the *Eldridge*, the other vessel, or somewhere else. Reportedly, Allende put his arm in the field up to his shoulder and this was the reason he suffered from a chronic arm ailment the rest of his life.

This is just about all the information the lady could remember. It does explain, or at least gives a possible theory, as to how Allende stumbled onto the information in the first place. Allende demonstrated an ability to retain complicated information that he most likely did not fully understand. As stated earlier in this text, this is a symptom of mind control. Allende held on to this information and began to release it in the famous "Allende letters" to Morris Jessup.

Obviously, there is a lot more information besides the above, but it seems that someone with access to the postal service went way out of their way to ensure that I did not learn anything further. The effort to "murder" the Philadelphia Experiment is apparently still in full force.

Fortunately, no matter how long it takes, the truth has a way of bobbing itself to the surface. Recently, Al Bielek put me in touch with a man who literally grew up at Brookhaven Labs, that mystery of mysteries which inherited the research from the Philadelphia Experiment and brought the Montauk Project into being. For many years, I have encouraged someone to come forth and write a book about Brookhaven. Finally, and at long last, an insider has stepped forward and has told his story. This gentleman, whose real name is Wade Gordon, was chosen as a young boy by one of the primary project directors of the time experiments at Brookhaven. This project director knew that he could not himself tell the details of his work during his lifetime. Accordingly, he chose a youngster to tell his story to so that it could eventually be delivered to posterity. I have read the story, and it is fascinating. It ties Roswell and Los Alamos to Brookhaven and thus Montauk. It even includes information about a hyperspace chamber that was used at Brookhaven to investigate the JFK assassination. As we step forward into the new millennium, there seems to be no limit on what will be discovered.

No matter how much we like or dislike it, there will always be setbacks and breakthroughs. It is sometimes very sad when we consider the fate of people like Phil Schneider and Morris Jessup who have died in the quest for truth. These people and others like them make it possible for us to learn the true nature of the world around us. Fortunately, life does not end with the extinction of a mere body. The quest for truth and the secret of life itself springs eternal. You are a part of it.

INDEX

244

The Brookhaven Connection
by Wade Gordon
Edited by Peter Moon

After the Philadelphia Experiment was conducted in 1943, massive research ensued to study the "human factor" involved in the warping of space-time. The site chosen for the majority of this work was at Brookhaven National Laboratories, the most secretive research facility in the nation and the top nuclear lab. It was from Brookhaven that the Montauk Project was launched.

Now, for the first time, a man of German descent who "grew up" at Brookhaven comes forward and tells some of the deepest secrets yet to come forward from Long Island. This story ties the crash at Roswell and MJ-12 to the early nuclear reserach at Brookhaven and the subsequent research at Montauk. Prominent in this story is the creation of a hyperspace chamber at Brookhaven which was used for time travel. The researchers even use this chamber to take a trip back to the JFK assasination in order to secure funding for their work.

In one of the biggest bombshells yet from Sky Books, *The Brookhaven Connection* brings us face to face with the alien equation and starts a new download of information.

THE BIGGEST
SECRET
EVER TOLD

The Montauk Project: Experiments In Time chronicles the most amazing and secretive research project in recorded history. Starting with the "Philadelphia Experiment" of 1943, the Office of Naval research employed Albert Einstein's Unified Field Theory in an attempt to make the *USS Eldridge*, a destroyer escort, invisible to radar. The *Eldridge* not only became invisible on radar screens — it disappeared from time and space as we know it with full scale teleportation of the ship and crew. "The Philadelphia Experiment" was a total disaster to the crew members aboard the *Eldridge*. Psychological disorders, physical trauma and even deaths were reported as a result of the experiment.

Forty years of massive research continued culminating in even more bizarre experiments that took place at Montauk Point, New York that actually tapped the powers of creation and manipulated time itself. *The Montauk Project* is a first hand account by Preston Nichols, a technician who worked on the project. He has survived threats and attempts to brainwash his memory of what occurred. A fascinating account of the research, including the technological applications of changing time itself are given for the first time, along with Preston's intriguing personal story.

■ ■ ■ ■

160 pages, illustrations, photos and diagrams......$15.95

THE ASTONISHING
SEQUEL ...

Montauk Revisited: Adventures in Synchronicity pursues the mysteries of time so intriguingly brought to light in *The Montauk Project: Experiments in Time.* *Montauk Revisited* unmasks the occult forces that were behind the science and technology used in the *Montauk Project.* An ornate tapestry is revealed which interweaves the mysterious associations of the Cameron clan with the genesis of American rocketry and the magick of Aleister Crowley, Jack Parsons and L. Ron Hubbard. Also included is the bizarre history of the electronic transistor and how it was developed by the E.T. Company, an apparent front for aliens.

Montauk Revisited carries forward with the Montauk investigation as Preston Nichols opens the door to Peter Moon and unleashes a host of incredible characters and new information. A startling scenario is depicted that reaches far beyond the scope of the first book.

    The Montauk Project opened up the mystery of all mysteries. This sequel accelerates the pursuit.

■ ■ ■ ■

249 pages, illustrations, photos and diagrams......$19.95

THE ULTIMATE PROOF

*P*yramids of Montauk: Explorations In Consciousness unveils the mysteries of Montauk Point and its select location for pyramids and time travel experimentation. An astonishing sequel to the *Montauk Project* and *Montauk Revisited*, this chapter of the legend awakens the consciousness of humanity to its ancient history and origins through the discovery of pyramids at Montauk. Their placement on sacred Native American ground opens the door to an unprecedented investigation of the mystery schools of Earth and their connection to Egypt, Atlantis, Mars and the star Sirius.

Preston Nichols continues to fascinate with an update on covert operations at Montauk Point that includes the discovery of a nuclear particle accelerator on the Montauk Base and the development of new psychotronic weapons.

Pyramids of Montauk propels us far beyond the adventures of the first two books and stirs the quest for future reality and the end of time as we know it.

▲ ▲ ▲ ▲

256 pages, illustrations, photos and diagrams......$19.95

MONTAUK'S
NAZI CONNECTION

In this spectacular addition to the Montauk series, *The Black Sun* continues the intriguing revelations readers have come to expect from Peter Moon as he digs deeper than ever before into the mysterious synchronicities that have made his work so popular.

The Black Sun is an adventure in consciousness revealing a vast array of new information. From the German flying saucer program to the SS Tibet mission, we are led on a path that gives us the most insightful look ever into the Third Reich and their ultimate quest: the Ark of the Covenant and the Holy Grail.

Going beyond *The Spear of Destiny* and other attempts to unlock the mysterious occultism of the Nazis, Peter Moon peers into the lab of the ancient alchemists and their white powdered gold in order to explain the secret meaning behind the Egyptian and Tibetan "Books of the Dead".

• • • • •

Journey to the stars–

with Preston Nichols & Peter Moon's

ENCOUNTER IN THE PLEIADES: AN INSIDE LOOK AT UFOS

*T*his is the incredible story of a man who found himself taken to the Pleiades where he was given a scientific education far beyond the horizons of anything taught in universities. For the first time, the personal history of Preston Nichols is revealed along with an avalanche of amazing information the world has not yet heard. A new look at Einstein and the history of physics gives unprecedented insight into the technology of flying saucers and their accompanying phenomena. Never before has the complex subject of UFOs been explained in such a simple language that will be appreciated by the scientist and understood by the layman.

Peter Moon adds further intrigue to the mix by divulging his part in a bizarre project which led him to Preston Nichols and the consequent release of this information. His account of the role of the Pleiades in ancient mythology sheds new light on the current predicament of Mankind and offers a path of hope for the future. The truth is revealed. The keys to the Pleiades are in hand and the gateway to the stars is open.   252 pages......$19.95

MONTAUK:
THE ALIEN CONNECTION
BY STEWART SWERDLOW
EDITED BY PETER MOON

Montauk: The Alien Connection reveals the most amazing story yet to surface in the area of alien abduction. This is an autobiographical and factual account from Stewart Swerdlow, a gifted mentalist who was born clairvoyant but haunted by strange time-space scenarios.

After suffering alien abductions and government manipulations, Stewart found Preston Nichols and discovered his own role in time travel experiments known as the Montauk Project. After refusing to break his association with Nichols, Stewart was incarcerated by the authorities, but the truth began to reveal itself. Struggling for his life, Stewart used his mental abilities to overcome the negative influences surrounding him and ultimately discovered the highest common denominator in the alien equation — an  interdimensional language which communicates to all conscious beings.

Montauk: The Alien Connection is an intriguing new twist to the Montauk saga which elevates the entire subject to a higher octave.

ISBN 0-9631889-8-4 , $19.95
Published by Sky Books, Box 769, Westbury, NY 11590

The Montauk Pulse™
A CHRONICLE OF TIME

A newsletter by the name of *The Montauk Pulse* went into print in the winter of 1993 to chronicle the events and discoveries regarding the ongoing investigation of the Montauk Project by Preston Nichols and Peter Moon. It has remained in print and been issued quarterly ever since. With a minimum of six pages and a distinct identity of its own, *The Pulse* will often comment on details and history that do not necessarily find their way into books.

Through 2000, The *Montauk Pulse* has included exciting new breakthroughs on the Montauk story as well as similarly related phenomena like the Philadelphia Experiment or other space-time projects. As of 2000, the scope of *The Pulse* will be expanded to embrace any new phenomena concerning any of the past books on Montauk as well as new developments on the Phil Schneider case and the mysteries concerning Brookhaven Labs.

Subscribing to *The Pulse* directly contributes to the efforts of the authors in writing more books and chronicling the effort to understand time and all of its components. We appreciate your support.

For a complimentary listing of
special interdimensional books and videos —
send a self-addressed, stamped #10 envelope to:
Sky Books, Box 769, Westbury, NY 11590-0104